THE PRUNING ANSWER BOOK

THE Pruning ANSWER BOOK

Solutions to Every Problem You'll Ever Face

Answers to Every Question You'll Ever Ask

LEWIS HILL & PENELOPE O'SULLIVAN

Storey Publishing

*The mission of Storey Publishing is to serve our customers by
publishing practical information that encourages
personal independence in harmony with the environment.*

Edited by Gwen Steege, Carleen Madigan, and Elizabeth P. Stell
Editorial adaptation by Penelope O'Sullivan
Art direction and book design by Cynthia N. McFarland
Text production by Jennifer Jepson Smith

Cover and interior decorative illustration by © William Howell Golson
Interior illustrations by © Elayne Sears, except for 167 by Beverly Duncan;
   42 top, 54, 56, 57, 81, 82, 138, 192–194, and 288 by Elara Tanguy

Indexed by Catherine F. Goddard
Expert review by Tchukki Andersen and Kevin Smith

Storey Publishing
210 MASS MoCA Way
North Adams, MA 01247
www.storey.com

Printed in China by Regent Publishing Services
10 9 8 7 6 5 4 3 2 1

LIBRARY OF CONGRESS CATALOGING-IN-PUBLICATION DATA

Hill, Lewis
  [Pruning made easy]
  The pruning answer book / Lewis Hill and Penelope O'Sullivan.
    p. cm.
  Previously published as: Pruning made easy.
  Includes index.
  ISBN 978-1-60342-710-4 (flexibind with paper spine : alk. paper)
  1. Pruning. I. O'Sullivan, Penelope. II. Title.
SB125H45 2011
635.9'1542—dc22

                      2010043058

Contents

Acknowledgments

Skillful editors make me a better writer. I thank Gwen Steege, who initiated this project; and Carleen Madigan and Liz Stell for working with me on this book. I'm grateful to Pam Art, Storey's president, and Deborah Balmuth, editorial director, for their support. Art director Cindy McFarland, Ilona Sherratt, and illustrators Elayne Sears and Elara Tanguy designed a book that's fun and easy to use, and Amy Greeman, publicity director, is promoting it. Special thanks go to Nancy Hill for trusting me to update the work of Lewis, her late husband.

My technical readers are the unsung heroes of this manuscript. Tchukki Andersen, consulting arborist for the Tree Care Industry Association in Londonderry, New Hampshire, commented with patience and knowledge. Kevin T. Smith, PhD, project leader and supervisory plant physiologist at the USDA Forest Service in Durham, New Hampshire, kept me on track when I ventured into tree science.

I'd also like to acknowledge some top-notch written resources: Edward F. Gilman's *An Illustrated Guide to Pruning*, 2nd edition; the late Alex L. Shigo's *Modern Arboriculture* and *Tree Pruning: A Worldwide Photo Guide*; and the websites www.treedictionary.com and www.invasive.org/species/list.cfm?id=76.

Pruning delights me whether I'm taking off suckers or watching arborists remove dead limbs from big trees. I thank my clients, friends, and husband (a keen plant collector), who let me hone my skills on their very special trees and shrubs.

They honor me with their confidence. My husband, Bob, showed love in action by cooking dinners and doing many of my chores while I wrote. I praise Leslie Webb, Candace Wheeler, Rose Matheny, and Daniela Kulik for centering me, and my kind neighbors and loving friends who cheer me on.

— *Penelope O'Sullivan*

Improving on Nature

Nature is a master gardener and pruner extraordinaire. Just visit an orchard in early summer. If the fruit set is unusually heavy, you'll see hundreds of little apples or peaches on the ground. Trees drop the extras when they lack the resources to develop them to maturity. And look around you in winter. Snow, high winds, and ice storms prune by snapping off weak old branches.

In gardens and in the wild, rabbits, mice, deer, elk, moose, beavers, and porcupines prune — just not in ways we consider horticultural achievements. They're eating at their favorite restaurants, but in doing so, they fit into the scheme of life. Let's face it: if you don't prune, Nature will! Over time, people have observed Nature's pruning methods and tried to improve on them because pruning — when properly done — strengthens rather than weakens trees. Here are the answers to your most pressing pruning questions. Pruning is a balance between art and science, between a plant's essential form and your pruning goal or the effect you want to achieve. Remember, a well-maintained landscape with handsome trees and shrubs brings pleasure to you and your neighbors, and adds value to your home and community.

CHAPTER 1

Why Prune?

Ever wrecked a tree or shrub by pruning it? The pruning fundamentals in this book can keep you from repeating the mistake. Knowing the basics boosts the beauty of your garden and helps your plants survive and thrive. Here are some of pruning's many benefits:

- Promoting health and vigor
- Keeping up appearances
- Enhancing natural form
- Showcasing beautiful bark
- Increasing flowering
- Increasing yields from fruit trees and berry bushes
- Controlling size
- Guiding growth
- Managing a view
- Mending damage
- Eliminating hazards

Pruning helps keeps woody plants healthy. Proper pruning can also enhance the natural pattern of growth of a shrub or tree, improve flowering and fruit set, and control its size. Sometimes you can prune out growth as preventative medicine or to eliminate a disease. Young or old trees and bushes may have problems that pruning can solve.

Promoting Health and Vigor

Q I have some tree and shrub plantings that grew well for a while, but now they don't look as good. Can pruning get them growing again?

A If a shrub or tree is beginning to show symptoms of age but is not quite ready to retire, pruning can restore vitality. Although you may be tempted to chop back every old plant to stimulate new growth, this doesn't always work. It is risky on large old shade trees. Broadleaf evergreens and conifers are also unlikely to benefit from severe beheading. Even if young and vigorous, a drastic slashing of a spruce or pine tree can prove fatal.

Yet some plants respond well to drastic, carefully considered techniques. In some regions of the country, certain roses (even old ones) may flower best only if you cut them back nearly to the ground each spring. And clematis, shrubby cinquefoil, hydrangea, lilac, and honeysuckle all seem to benefit from occasional drastic pruning. A young, forked tree can often be shaped into a strong, straight specimen by cutting off one of the forks and staking the other. In time, the crook in the stem will straighten.

Most berry-producing ornamentals, on the other hand, such as cotoneaster and viburnum, need little or no pruning. Older trees and bushes prefer rejuvenation by light and frequent pruning.

SEE ALSO: *Pages 100–101 for renewing old shrubs.*

Q I'm confused about what I should remove to keep my plants strong. Can you give me some basic guidelines for pruning my trees and shrubs?

A In general, regular pruning that begins early in a plant's life is less of a shock to the plant and also always looks better than a full-scale attack with shears and saw. For instance, orchardists renew the bearing wood on their fruit trees gradually by removing some older branches each year. This method is also best for bush fruits such as blueberries and gooseberries. The bearing is uninterrupted, regrowth is moderate, and the bush or tree suffers no serious setbacks. The same is true for ornamentals.

To maintain healthy plants, remove (**1**) diseased growth, (**2**) branches too close to ground, (**3**) dead branches, (**4**) crossing and rubbing branches, (**5**) water sprouts, and (**6**) suckers.

What steps should I take to prune for a healthier tree?

 If you see that a plant is struggling, step in to help.

1. Get rid of obvious problems first. Unlike injured animals that heal and repair, wounded trees wall off damage and grow parts in new places. To promote tree health, prune dead or damaged branches to just outside the branch collar (see page 62) on the trunk or on a main limb.

2. Eliminate stems, twigs, and branches that are diseased or infested with borers, scales, and other insects. Burn debris or bury deeply so the problem won't spread.

3. Remove suckers, or little trees, sprouting from the trunk or the roots. These deplete a tree's energy. If you allow them to grow, they will spoil your tree's appearance and turn it into a large bush. Unchecked suckers growing from the wild rootstock of a grafted fruit, shade tree, or rosebush can crowd out the desirable part of the plant.

4. Bark damage occurs when the branches of trees, especially deciduous ones, rub against buildings or other branches. To remedy, snip off offending limbs at a side branch or at the branch collar as soon as you see them. If you do nothing, branches may suffer bark damage, which invites infection and can lead to tree loss.

5. Remove water sprouts (branches growing straight up, often from old pruning scars) as soon as they form.

These branches weaken a tree and cause ugly growth that is difficult to deal with later.

6. Deal with like-size adjoining trunks with bark squeezed in the crotch between them by removing one of the trunks. A weak crotch can mean a cracked or broken trunk later on in the tree's life.

7. Prune fruit trees for increased air circulation and sunlight. Too-warm or too-cool temperatures and high humidity may lead to problems. You can prevent these by removing superfluous branches to admit moving air and light into the tree's interior.

Q I just moved from Boston to Miami. Will that change the way I prune?

A Gardeners in warmer parts of the country and in tropical and semitropical climates can do more severe pruning than those in cooler areas (except on conifers). Fast regrowth almost always follows a major pruning job in warm climates, while in the North, the soft, new growth may not completely harden before autumn frosts begin. Winter injury results, and a tree, already weakened by abnormal pruning and regrowth, may be damaged permanently or killed outright.

Keeping Up Appearances

Q How do I know if my trees and shrubs need to be pruned?

A Pruning is both art and science. Maintaining an appealing landscape in proportion to your house is as important as keeping your plants healthy and strong. That's where directing plant growth through smart pruning comes in.

New plants grow so slowly that they usually need little pruning the first few years. Suddenly, though, they begin to grow rapidly, and soon they become too large. Ask yourself:

♦ Are the proportions right?
♦ Do the shapes complement each other?

Some landscapers like their work to look finished the day they put in the plants. To accomplish this they use more and bigger plants than necessary, meaning that after a few years, everything is crowded. When this occurs, remove the extras instead of cutting them back.

Pruning for appearance involves much more than just controlling plant size. It also means keeping evergreens and flowering shrubs well proportioned, removing sucker growth from the bottoms of trees, and taking off limbs or blooms that detract from a plant's appearance. Prune in relation to the rest of the planting, the house, other buildings, walks, and walls. Keep your plantings attractive but not so showy that they hide or detract from your home. The landscape should look nice from both inside and outside the house.

Q My evergreens have grown so tall that they block my view of a neighboring pond. I don't want to cut them down, so what can I do?

A Gardeners prune for many reasons, from improving the health and productivity of plantings to manipulating an entire view. Create sight lines by limbing up particular trees, thus opening distant views for your pleasure. Conversely, you can block ugliness from sight with a dense evergreen screen.

SEE ALSO: *Limbing Up, page 64.*

Q What mistakes can pruning help correct?

A Among these problems are (**1**) improper placement of shrubs, (**2**) spreading evergreens that crowd a path, (**3**) doorway plantings that have grown too large, (**4**) foundation plants that crowd each other, (**5**) foundation plantings that hide windows, (**6**) a shade tree in front of and too close to the house, and (**7**) flowering shrubs that hide rather than frame the house.

Enhancing Natural Form

Q Is there a rule of thumb for training and shaping trees and shrubs?

A Let nature guide you, and prune to enhance your plant's natural form. To avoid making major pruning mistakes when training a young tree, study its mature shape in a picture, a neighbor's yard, or a public garden.

Let trees that grow in a pyramidal or columnar form keep their lower branches. Spreading and rounded trees look better and are more useful as shade trees if you remove their bottom limbs. Prevent limbs of weeping deciduous trees from flopping on the ground.

WHAT'S IN A NAME?

Some horticultural names give you a clue about a plant's growth habit. When you see 'Fastigiata', 'Columnare', or 'Erecta', you can be sure the tree will take on an erect, upright form. 'Pyramidalis' indicates a cone shape. 'Globosa', like globe, naturally indicates a round shape. 'Nana' means dwarf, and 'Pendula' refers to a hanging or weeping growth habit.

Q Can pruning change the long, thin shape of a dogwood that I planted under some oak trees?

A Thinning the oaks' canopies to let more light reach the dogwood might help. Light conditions and growing space affect a tree's mature form. Trees grown in full sun and open space are fuller with more branches, leaves, flowers, and fruits than their shaded counterparts because sunlight is the main source of a tree's food and energy. Shaded trees have less exposure to sunlight, thus fewer leaves to manufacture food. Trees growing in crowded conditions tend to shade each other out. Growth tends to be narrow and stretched upward toward the sun. Find out whether your trees and shrubs need full sun or if they will tolerate some shade.

Q Do I need to prune my ornamental crab apple?

A It depends. If your goal is a tree with a full, handsome crown, you may need to do very little to keep it looking great. Prune sparingly, removing only damaged or weak wood, branches that are crossing or rubbing others, and the occasional branch that shoots off in an odd direction. Many varieties become beautiful specimens with very little intervention. If enjoying flowers is your primary goal, prune right after the flowers fade.

SEE ALSO: *Flowering Trees, page 94.*

NATURAL FORMS OF TREES

Good pruning respects a tree's natural shape, including the distinctive shapes of the trees listed here. Do you recognize your tree's shape below?

Columnar

Columnar European hornbeam (*Carpinus betulus* 'Columnaris')
Columnar sugar maple (*Acer saccharum* 'Newton Sentry')
Dawyck European beech (*Fagus sylvatica* 'Dawyckii')
Fastigiate Swiss stone pine (*Pinus cembra* 'Fastigiata')
Lombardy poplar (*Populus nigra* 'Italica')
Pyramid arborvitae (*Thuja occidentalis* 'Pyramidalis')
Sky Pencil Japanese holly (*Ilex crenata* 'Sky Pencil')
Skyrocket juniper (*Juniperus scopulorum* 'Skyrocket')
Some colonnade-style apples (*Malus* 'Scarlet Sentinel', M. 'Golden Sentinel', M. 'Maypole', M. 'Northpole', M. 'Crimson Spire', M. 'Emerald Spire', M. 'Scarlet Spire', M. 'Ultra Spire')
Upright English oak (*Quercus robur* 'Fastigiata')
Upright European beech (*Fagus sylvatica* 'Fastigiata')
Upright mountain ash (*Sorbus aucuparia* 'Fastigiata')
Upright white pine (*Pinus strobus* 'Fastigiata')

columnar

Pyramidal

Alder (*Alnus* spp.)
American arborvitae (*Thuja occidentalis*)
American holly (*Ilex opaca*)
Bald cypress (*Taxodium distichum*)
Black gum (*Nyssa sylvatica*), when young
Douglas fir (*Pseudotsuga menziesii*)
English holly (*Ilex aquifolium*)

Fir (*Abies* spp.)
Larch (*Larix* spp.)
Spruce (*Picea* spp.)
Sweetbay magnolia (*Magnolia virginiana*)
True cedar (*Cedrus* spp.)
Turkish filbert (*Corylus colurna*)
Upright yew (*Taxus cuspidata*)

pyramidal

Rounded

Cornelian cherry dogwood (*Cornus mas*)
European hornbeam (*Carpinus betulus*)
Fox Valley river birch (*Betula nigra* 'Little King')
Japanese hemlock (*Isuga diversifolia*)
Japanese maple (*Acer palmatum*)
Kousa dogwood (*Cornus kousa*)
Red buckeye (*Aesculus pavia*)
Round-leafed European beech (*Fagus sylvatica*
  'Rotundifolia')
Sargent crab apple (*Malus sargentii*)
Umbrella catalpa (*Catalpa bignonioides* 'Nana')

round

Spreading

Amur cork tree (*Phellodendron amurense*)
Basswood (*Tilia americana*)
European beech (*Fagus sylvatica*)
Ginkgo (*Ginkgo biloba*) with age
Honey locust (*Gleditsia triacanthos* var. *inermis*)
Katsura (*Cercidiphyllum japonicum*) with age
Live oak (*Quercus virginiana*)
London plane tree (*Platanus* × *acerifolia*)
Saucer magnolia (*Magnolia* × *soulangiana*)
Sweet birch (*Betula lenta*) with age
White oak (*Quercus alba*)

spreading

Weeping

Golden weeping willow (*Salix × sepulcralis* 'Chrysocoma')
Weeping Eastern hemlock (*Tsuga canadensis* 'Pendula')
Weeping European beech (*Fagus sylvatica* 'Pendula')
Weeping Higan cherry (*Prunus subhirtella* 'Pendula')
Weeping katsura (*Cercidiphyllum japonicum* 'Pendulum')
Weeping larch (*Larix decidua* 'Pendula')
Weeping Norway spruce (*Picea abies* 'Pendula')
Weeping white pine (*Pinus strobus* 'Pendula')
Weeping willow (*Salix babylonica*)

weeping

Vase-Shaped

Hackberry (*Celtis occidentalis*) when young
Japanese zelkova (*Zelkova serrulata*)
Kwanzan flowering cherry (*Prunus* 'Kwanzan')
Paperbark maple (*Acer griseum*) with age
Valley Forge American elm (*Ulmus americana* 'Valley Forge'), a cultivar resistant to Dutch elm disease

vase

Q My river birch clump has gorgeous peeling bark,
but you can't see it when the tree's in leaf. How can
I show off the texture of the bark?

A Try cutting off limbs at the base of the tree (known
as limbing up or basal pruning, page 64). In addition
to showing off the bark, removing lower limbs opens up living or planting space under large trees, frames views, and lets
light into dark spots.

TREES WITH COLORFUL OR STRIKING BARK

These handsome trees are good candidates for
limbing up.

Lacebark elm (*Ulmus parvifolia*)
Lacebark pine (*Pinus bungeana*)
London plane tree (*Platanus* × *hispanica*)
Madrone (*Arbutus menziesii*)
Paper birch (*Betula papyrifera*)
River birch (*Betula nigra*)
Snakebark maple (*Acer capillipes*)
Stewartia (*Stewartia* spp.)

Improving Flowering and Fruiting

Q Will pruning help my camellia to produce larger flowers?

A If you remove some of the buds, you'll get fewer blooms but each one will be larger. This technique is called *disbudding*. Camellias are frequently disbudded in late August and September to increase flower size and quality. To accomplish this, leave one bud per terminal, though this may differ according to the age, size, and type of camellia you're disbudding.

SEE ALSO: *Page 116 for disbudding roses.*

Q Do I prune my 'Liberty' apple tree the same as my ornamental crab apple?

A Yes and no. With either tree, you'll want to remove dead and damaged wood. Prune your apple — and other trees grown primarily for edible fruits — to ensure a plentiful harvest. Take off a couple old limbs each year. That way, you can renew the fruit-bearing branches in six to eight years. Remove water sprouts, those upright, vigorous-growing branches that cause unwanted shade and are usually unproductive. Also remove the extra fruits when your tree sets too many. Thinning fruits makes the remaining ones grow bigger and better.

SEE ALSO: *Pruning Fruit Trees, pages 213–266.*

Controlling Size

Q Help! My trees and shrubs are overwhelming the house. Can pruning help me control their size?

A A good planting connects the house to the land, provides an attractive setting, and gives the yard a finished look. Although it's always best to grow trees and shrubs that mature to a suitable size, pruning helps keep too-big plants in check. For example, hemlock or arborvitae trees that might otherwise grow 40 to 80 feet tall can be maintained as a much shorter hedge by regular shearing. Pruning may be necessary for large trees and bushes that crowd power lines, driveways, sidewalks, or buildings.

Well-pruned ornamentals enhance the appearance of a house.

Q Are there ways to control size without pruning?

A Yes! Consider these alternatives to pruning to reduce the time and cost of maintenance:

♦ Read labels and buy plants that mature to the desired size for a particular location. Consider varieties of fruits, evergreens, and shrubs that are labeled dwarf. Even these may require some control or they'll eventually outgrow their space.

♦ Plant fruits or ornamentals in large tubs placed on a patio, deck, or terrace. Confining the roots helps limit plant size, so you won't have to prune as much.

Guiding Growth

Q I planted a climbing hydrangea near a tree, a few feet from the trunk where I want it to grow. How do I get the vine off the ground and up the tree?

A Guiding plant growth takes some pruning and patience. For your climbing hydrangea (*H. anomala* subsp. *petiolaris*), take some long stems and tie them loosely to the tree with string. You may have to do this in more than one place on the trunk, depending on the length of the stems you're attaching. Remove the twine once the rootlets begin to attach themselves to the trunk. Climbing hydrangea also makes a lovely mounding ground cover. To control its spread, cut back wayward stems when dormant.

Q Can early training increase the life span of a tree?

A You can sometimes prevent injury by pruning for a strong structure early in a tree's life. This task is especially important if you want to grow brittle-wooded trees such as willows and silver maples. Strong limbs usually connect to trunks at angles greater than 45 degrees and less than 90 degrees and have no included bark (bark wedged inside where the branch attaches). If your tree has included bark, narrow crotches can promote limb failure. When your tree is young, you can remove branches with skinny V-crotches or use spreaders to widen them.

SEE ALSO: *Training Shade Trees, page 80.*

Mending Damage

Q Last winter an ice storm tore some limbs off a willow. Do we have to take it out?

A If the trunk and most limbs survived, then try to improve the tree's looks with pruning. Prune off broken limbs at the branch collar soon after the injury occurs. Jagged stubs give disease-causing pathogens easy access to a tree. Disease weakens a tree and makes it susceptible to pest infestations, which may lead to even more problems. You may have to wait a few years until the tree recovers some vitality to reshape it. Do that during dormancy, and never remove more than 25 percent of the canopy in any one year (10 to 15 percent is better).

Eliminating Hazards

Q We installed creeping junipers in our front-entry beds. Now the branches cover more than half the front path. What should I do?

A Safety first; you don't want to hurt yourself or your visitors! Cut back the junipers so family and friends can walk unobstructed on the path. If you don't want to keep up with the pruning, consider moving them to a larger space and replacing them with a less vigorous ground cover.

Pruning for safety is also necessary around power lines, windows, doors, and wherever damaged limbs or trunks endanger the well-being of people and your home. Never prune around electrical or utility lines yourself; contact your utility or municipality or hire a qualified arborist.

Q How can I reduce the chance of a tree falling on my house?

A Some fast-growing, brittle trees such as silver maple (*Acer saccharinum*) and tulip tree (*Liriodendron tulipifera*) have thick crowns that develop a sail-like wind resistance, making them poor candidates for surviving high winds intact. You can improve the odds for these and similar trees by removing limbs with narrow crotch angles and selectively thinning the crown to reduce wind resistance.

CHAPTER 2

When to Prune

Ask a hundred gardeners "When is the best time to prune?" and you may get a hundred answers. Some highly respected nurserymen and academics maintain that the best time is whenever your plants need the attention and you have the time to do the job. Often, however, the answer depends on a plant's condition, the length of the growing season, and your pruning goals — do you want maximum flowering or damage repair? Give your plants a touch-up or take off a dead, sick, or broken limb as needed, but wait until dormancy for more extensive pruning.

Q When's the best time to prune my trees and shrubs?

A Because of the tremendous difference in weather conditions throughout the continent, it is difficult to give precise directions on exactly when to prune. See individual chapters for more specific advice for different types of trees and shrubs.

SEE ALSO: *Plant-by-Plant Pruning Guide, starting on page 311.*

Q Why should I prune in winter to early spring?

A Most gardeners like to do major pruning on their trees and shrubs when they're dormant, in late winter or early spring. The time is just before the surge of new spring growth, when deciduous branches are bare, so it's easy to see what you're doing. Since "late winter" and "early spring" mean a different time in each locale, take it to mean whenever the days begin to lengthen but before the ground warms up, the buds swell, and new growth begins.

Although late-winter pruning encourages fast regrowth of wood, avoid taking off too many leafy branches in one season. Some experts say you can remove up to 25 percent of the crown in a year without harming a tree (depending on the species). However, 10 to 15 percent is better, because too much pruning weakens trees, particularly old ones. Removing too many branches may cause profuse suckers and water sprouts to grow, signs of a tree under stress or in decline.

Make cuts just to the outside of the branch collar to allow the tree to seal over as well as possible. Large pruning cuts take a lot of energy for the tree to deal with, so make sure you avoid making too many large cuts on one plant in the same season.

SAPPY TREES

Some trees appear to "bleed" a lot of sap if pruned in early spring. Don't worry if you see sap running from the cuts on maples, birches, willows, walnuts, beeches, hornbeams, and yellowwoods pruned at this time. They're not bleeding, and sap flow won't hurt them. If you prefer to wait until less sap is flowing, prune in midsummer. Before pruning in summer, though, check first with your local Cooperative Extension Service to ensure that summer pruning is not harmful to your particular species. For example, don't prune white-barked birches — which are more susceptible to bronze birch borers than other birches are — between May and September, when these insects are flying.

Q What are the best plants to prune in late winter to early spring?

A You can prune flowering trees, fruit trees, woody vines, conifers, and broadleaf evergreens. However, late-winter pruning reduces the number of blossoms on spring-flowering trees and shrubs, so delay pruning these until right after flowering if maximum bloom is your goal. Most roses do well when pruned in very early spring, around the time the forsythia blooms.

Q Why prune trees and shrubs when dormant?

A Plant dormancy is a type of hibernation that occurs in late fall and lasts into early spring, before growth starts. In late fall, deciduous plants have dropped their leaves and stopped growing aboveground. Underground plant growth slows but continues until halted by deep ground frost. In dormancy, you can see the form of deciduous plants and correct disease, insect, and shearing damage. Also, you can take advantage of a plant's spring growth spurt to cover pruning cuts and hasten the plant's recovery. Dormancy is also a good time to thin broadleaved evergreens and let more light into the canopy of deciduous trees.

Q Can I prune trees after they leaf out in spring?

A Enjoy your trees in spring, but don't prune them when actively growing in mid-spring. Aside from removing dead or damaged wood, pruning trees during their major growth spurt brings such unwanted results as increased suckers.

Pruning trees after the spring growth flush reduces their growth rate, which is useful to control plant size. It's also a good time to prune hedges, since new growth will be slowed. Why the slowdown? You're decreasing the tree's leafy space, and thus lowering the food production needed for robust growth.

Q Which trees and shrubs do I prune in late spring and summer?

A Prune spring-flowering plants that bloom on old wood, such as dogwood, lilac, bridal wreath, and spring-blossoming spirea, immediately after blooming. You can enjoy their flowering, and they can develop a new set of buds for the next spring. Prune oakleaf and bigleaf hydrangeas when the flowers fade. If you see broken branches needing removal, it's okay to take them off. You can also shear evergreen hedges and prune conifers right after spring growth occurs.

Q Late summer and fall are great times to work outdoors. What can I prune at this time?

A Avoid pruning woody plants in late summer and early fall, since plants are particularly susceptible to fungal diseases at this time. Also, new growth may not have time to harden before cold weather arrives. This practice can result in winter injury that needs correcting with additional pruning in spring. By November, woody plants will probably be dormant and you can do corrective pruning by removing dead, diseased, and damaged material.

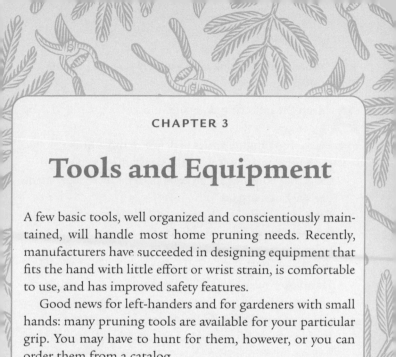

CHAPTER 3

Tools and Equipment

A few basic tools, well organized and conscientiously maintained, will handle most home pruning needs. Recently, manufacturers have succeeded in designing equipment that fits the hand with little effort or wrist strain, is comfortable to use, and has improved safety features.

Good news for left-handers and for gardeners with small hands: many pruning tools are available for your particular grip. You may have to hunt for them, however, or you can order them from a catalog.

Q What should I think about when I buy my pruning tools?

A Keep the following points in mind:

- **Price.** Tool quality varies widely. For most home gardening you won't need the heavy-duty, expensive tools that commercial growers prefer, but cheaply made tools are no bargain.

- **Feel.** If possible, test how a tool feels in your hand before buying. Ask yourself: Is it too heavy, too light, too large, or too small? Squeeze it to see if it is comfortable for your hand, wrist, and arm.

- **Hand or power tool?** Using power tools is a matter of personal preference. If you do lots of shearing and pruning, try electric hedge shears and power saws. People who love motors and expensive gadgets will also buy power equipment; those who prefer the economy and quiet of hand tools will prefer manual equipment.

- **Buy the right size tool for the job.** Suit the handle length of pruners and loppers to the diameter of the stems you'll be cutting. Longer handles give you more leverage and are thus better for cutting larger branches.

- **Advice.** Ask gardening friends which tools they use, for what, and why.

Pruners and Loppers

Q What's the best tool to carry when I'm walking around the garden and see a stray stem that needs trimming?

A Hand clippers, pruners, or snips, as they are variously called, work well for most small pruning jobs. Choose a quality product. Cheap ones don't hold up well with repeated use and make uneven cuts. Hand pruners range from about 7 to 9 inches long and work on stems up to ¾ inch in diameter. They come in two styles: bypass and anvil.

If you want only one hand pruner, choose the bypass style. These scissors-type pruners allow a sharp blade to move past an edged blade. They are more flexible for garden use because they cut cleaner and can cut closer than the anvil in narrow branch angles. Keep the cutting blade extra sharp, because you will use this tool for final cuts that shape the plant and contribute to its well-being.

bypass pruners

Anvil pruners crush the stem because they employ a sharp blade that hits squarely against a flat metal surface (an "anvil"). This is good for brush clearing, deadwood, and cutting up kindling. Use it where removal, not a clean cut, is your priority. You can also use anvil pruners to make preliminary cuts when doing fine pruning of shrubs and trees.

anvil pruners

Q What do I use to trim branches that are too far inside a shrub to reach with hand pruners?

A If you have high shrubbery or fruit trees, you'll also need loppers (two-handed pruners with long handles). They cut branches up to 1½ inches in diameter. Choose a well-made tool that won't break on the heavier jobs. Some have compound levers for extra-heavy work, and you'll find these especially useful for cutting brush or thinning out excessive growth, such as when taming an overgrown lilac. Long-handled loppers provide more leverage than do hand clippers.

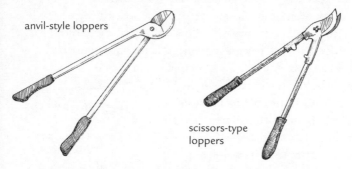

anvil-style loppers

scissors-type loppers

WHEN TO CALL IN THE PROS

Pruning tall trees and large limbs is dangerous. If you have to use a heavy chain saw or a cherry picker or climb trees and tall ladders to remove branches, hire professionals to do the job.

Q How do I prune a branch in a tree without using a ladder?

A The hand pruner has also been developed into a pole pruner, incorporating a set of extensions that enable you to reach farther up into a tree. It cuts branches up to 1½ inches across. The blade is activated by pulling on a rope that, when released, allows the blade to return to its normal position by the action of a strong spring. Pole pruners are handy for a lot of high work, especially in places where the use of a ladder would be difficult or dangerous. Do not use them near power lines.

Q How do I maintain my tools from day to day?

A Here's how:

◆ Carry a rag in your pocket when gardening and wipe the blades of hand pruners after use.

◆ After pruning, clean sticky sap and bits of bark or wood from saw blades and pruners.

◆ If you use your tools on evergreens, regularly clean off the pitch deposits. A citrus solvent will do the trick.

◆ After cleaning, apply an occasional drop of light motor oil or lubricating oil to the moving parts of pruners, loppers, hedge shears, and electric clippers to keep them operating well.

◆ To keep saws and metal blades rust-free, wipe them with a soft cloth dipped in light oil before you put them away. Do this little chore without fail before you store the tools each winter.

◆ Periodically take apart clippers and hedge shears to clean, sharpen, and oil.

Q After using my hand pruner, it gets dull and doesn't cut well. Besides replacing the cutting blade, how can I keep my pruner sharp?

A Sharp tools make clean cuts that heal quickly. Keeping them in good condition is easy and well worth the effort. Sharpen your pruner's blades with a grindstone, carborundum stone, whetstone, or steel file. Here's how:

1. Take apart the tool with care, lining up parts in the order you remove them so that reassembly won't baffle you. Wipe them off with a rag soaked in paint thinner, and then use a razor blade to scrape off any residue that remains.

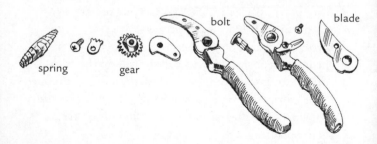

spring   gear   bolt   blade

2. Lubricate the sharpening stone with a light coating of oil. Affix the blade to the handle and, holding the partially reassembled tool at an angle, lay the beveled edge flat against the stone and pull it toward you. As you work, the edge should become even and shiny.

Q Do I need any special safety equipment when pruning?

A Yes, you should protect your hands, eyes, and head:

◆ **Wear heavy gloves** to prevent blisters and to protect your hands. Gloves are also useful when you need to move heavy or thorny limbs or evergreen brush.

◆ **Wear plastic safety goggles** to protect your eyes from sharp twigs, snapped-back branches, and flying debris.

◆ **Wear a hard hat** or a motorcycle, snowmobile, or bike helmet for added protection when using pole pruners and when sawing off limbs over your head.

GENERAL PRUNING-TOOL SAFETY

Although most pruning is not hazardous, it would be embarrassing to shift from performing surgery on a tree to having some performed on yourself. Keep the following safety pointers in mind:

◆ Use only sharp tools, and use the right-size tool for the job. You'll use less effort, and the resulting clean cuts on the plants will heal faster.

◆ Use a ladder only for small trees, and only for light pruning. Make sure the ladder is stable and secure. Pruning from a ladder is dangerous and can lead to serious injury. Hire a professional arborist for tall trees and large limbs.

◆ Avoid using electrical tools such as hedge clippers during or directly after rain. Wear rubber boots for insulation when the ground is even a little wet. Fiberglass ladders are safer around electrical equipment than are those made of metal.

◆ Never prune near electrical or utility wires. Contact your city, town, or utility company to do the job. Avoid using metal pole pruners or aluminum ladders anywhere near overhead power lines.

Q What kind of shoes should I wear when I climb a tree?

A Climbing large trees, especially to remove large limbs, is best left to professionals. But if you ever decide to climb a small fruit tree, choosing shoes with rubber or plastic soles is less harmful to the tree — and you — than climbing in leather ones that might slip. And, of course, never wear lineman's spikes or hobnailed shoes while climbing a valuable tree; the sharp points could injure the bark.

Q I keep losing my pruning tools because I don't know where they're stored. How can I keep track of them when they're not in use?

A Hang tools on a pegboard or plywood sheet with a drawing or outline to indicate which tool goes where. This organized system makes it easy to identify missing tools and helps to ensure that they won't be left outside during a rain shower or overnight.

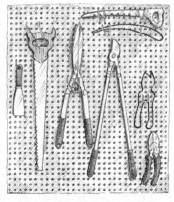

Before winter, it is important to store your tools properly so they will be in good shape for spring. Clean, sharpen, and oil all metal parts. Hang everything possible on nails or pegs on a wall. Never leave tools or equipment outdoors overnight or exposed to rain.

Saws

Q When should I use a saw?

A Use a pruning saw on any limb over ¾ inch in diameter. Heavy-duty, long-handled pruners, even those with compound levers, can squeeze the limb being cut, straining the tool and damaging the bark. For all heavy work, use a pruning saw.

Q There are so many saws for sale. Which type is best for pruning?

A For gardeners with light to average amounts of pruning, a curved-blade saw is versatile. Many gardeners prefer folding pull-stroke pruning saws because they're easy to carry and easy to use. They are ideal for many garden jobs and come with blades ranging from 6 to 24 inches long. A 6-inch blade can typically prune a branch up to 2 inches in diameter. Or try a lightweight bow saw; it is fast, easy to use, and handy in a woodlot.

Carpenter's saws are not effective on live wood, since they gum up and stick too much.

folding pruning saw

curved-blade pruning saw

Q What is a pole saw? What do I use it for?

A A pole saw is long-handled tree saw. Pole saws give you extra reach to let you prune small to medium branches while standing securely on terra firma, but they can be slow and laborious to use.

Q Which is better, a fine-toothed saw or a coarse-toothed?

A Use a fine-toothed saw for smooth branches up to 2½ inches in diameter and a coarse-toothed saw for large limbs 3 inches or more across. You may want one of each if you do a lot of pruning. Or choose a saw with two edges, one with coarse teeth and the other with fine.

Q Can I use a chain saw to prune my trees and shrubs?

A Chain saws are useful for removing and cutting up entire trees and for sawing off large limbs, but most are designed more for cutting wood or lumber than for pruning. They tend to make rough cuts, and they're difficult to control for precision work. Even if a chain saw is small, it is extremely easy to slash into the wrong limb, scar the trunk, or do other damage when you're pruning a tree with limbs that are close together.

CHAIN-SAW SAFETY

A chain saw is the most dangerous kind of pruning equipment. Both expert and amateur woodsmen have serious accidents while using them. Hiring a professional arborist is the best way to deal with major pruning, but if you choose to do otherwise, then be careful and follow these guidelines:

◆ Wear plastic safety goggles to protect your eyes from sawdust and bits of debris.

◆ Avoid making the type of cuts that pinch the saw or cause it to kick back.

◆ Keep the saw a safe distance from your body at all times.

◆ Do not use a chain saw while standing on a ladder.

◆ Never use a chain saw when you're tired.

◆ Always keep your chain saw sharpened — a dull saw is dangerous. Unless you are trained in sharpening these tools, leave the job to an expert. You can usually find a sharpener by looking in local newspapers or the phone directory. Hardware stores sometimes offer this service.

Hedge Shears, Clippers, and Knives

Q Can I use the same tools for pruning and shearing?

A No. Shearing, a form of pruning, involves removing soft new growth in order to get a tree to grow into a certain shape. Shearing is done primarily to shape hedges or to develop formal or topiary shrubbery. Because shearing does not involve cutting heavy wood, you will need different equipment from what you use for regular pruning.

Q What's my best choice for shearing a few bushes?

A Long-handled hedge shears are safe, durable, easy to control, and inexpensive. They suffice for most shearing jobs, are easily sharpened, and require little muscle power. Some are available with extra-long handles, making them especially good for high work such as reaching the top of a hedge.

long-handled hedge shears

Q What are the pros and cons of using a machete and knives to shear?

A Instead of hedge shears or electric clippers, some gardeners prefer to use a light, fast, thin-bladed machete called a shearing knife. It's popular with Christmas-tree growers and foresters because it's lightweight, easy, and fast to use. A shearing knife also has the advantage of being cheap, durable, and easy to keep sharpened. It is very useful on hedges, windbreaks, and overgrown thickets. Because the blade is long, this tool is not the best choice in close work, such as shearing miniature evergreens.

A major drawback is that a machete is hazardous. You must be extremely careful not to slice yourself. Professionals wear heavy gloves and leg guards or very thick pants. For safety's sake, keep a pair of hand clippers or a sharpening stone in the left hand while shearing with the right (or the reverse if you're left-handed) to avoid the dangerous temptation to hold up a limb in front of the knife. It sounds something like preventing a smashed thumb by holding the hammer in both hands while driving nails, but it works.

SHEARING-TOOL SAFETY

Follow these tips to stay safe when using gas-powered or electric-powered hedge shears:

- Make sure that electrical tools have the Underwriters Laboratory Seal of Approval.
- Be careful to keep blades away from your arms and legs when operating the tool.
- Don't let the cord get in the way while you're working to avoid snipping it off with the shrubbery.
- To prevent accidentally cutting the electrical cord, enclose the 2 feet nearest to the clippers in a piece of ½-inch plastic pipe, taping it in place so it won't slip.
- Keep shears well oiled at all times so that they run smoothly and don't overheat.

Q Formal hedges surround my property. What should I use to prune them?

A For extensive hedge shearing, electric shears are worth the price. These shears or clippers vary from small, light, inexpensive models to the heavy-duty kind necessary for rugged work. Base your choice on what type of hedge you have. Small, lightweight models are suitable for most deciduous plants. Coarse-twigged evergreens need shears that open wide enough to make clean cuts.

Consider buying a cordless model. These come with rechargeable batteries that eliminate the nuisance of a long electrical cord.

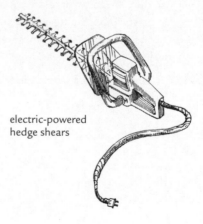

electric-powered
hedge shears

CHAPTER 4

Pruning Practices Right and Wrong

This chapter introduces the basic pruning cuts and techniques. You'll find the best place on a stem to cut and how to direct growth with strategically located cuts. Techniques consist of pinching (removing a bud or soft shoot or stem tip by squeezing it between thumb and forefinger); heading back (cutting back a branch to a side bud or lateral branch); thinning (pruning branches back to the trunk, to a big side branch, or to the ground to shrink the mass of a shrub, tree, or vine); root pruning (cutting straight down around a plant's root zone with a sharp spade); limbing up (removing the lowest branches and root suckers on a tree); and shearing (removing some of a plant's surface vegetation with shears).

You'll also discover techniques to avoid: topping — reducing the height of a tree by cutting big vertical limbs at right angles to their growth, usually between growth nodes — which destroys a tree's form and health; and tipping, similar to topping but it involves decreasing a tree's width by cutting lateral (side) branches at the wrong point.

UNDERSTANDING HOW PLANTS GROW

Before you start pruning, it helps to understand how woody plants grow. Trees and shrubs have growth sites (meristems) at their tips where cells divide and the new cells expand. The canopies of trees and shrubs grow taller and wider from these growing branch tips. Although other, reserve buds form along a branch, the bud at the tip (terminal bud) is by far the most vigorous. Through a hormonal process known as apical dominance, the terminal bud checks the growth of buds below it. Thus, if you cut off a branch tip (thereby eliminating the growth-regulating terminal bud), a bunch of vigorous shoots will grow from side (lateral) buds below the slice. In essence, you diverted energy from the tip to buds farther down the limb. Similarly, a trunk's diameter spreads by expansion of another growth site (vascular cambium) just under the bark, which adds a new layer of wood to the inside of the bark each year — hence, the rings on a log that enable you to determine a tree's age.

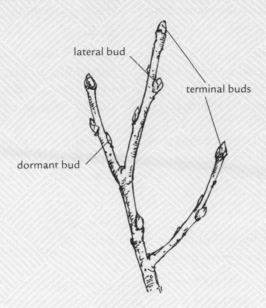

lateral bud

terminal buds

dormant bud

- ◆ **Terminal buds** are found at the top of a plant and at the ends of its branches.
- ◆ **Lateral (side) buds** form along the limbs.
- ◆ **Dormant (internodal) buds** are less obvious, tiny buds along the bud branches and sometimes under the bark. These are reserve buds, the plant's insurance policy. They will grow only if something happens to the regular buds. Most garden and forest shrubs and trees have them.

Where to Cut and Why

Q What do the words *thinning* and *heading back* mean?

A Heading back is removing only part of a branch, typically cutting back to a healthy outward-facing bud or branch. Thinning is cutting off an entire stem, either back to a larger branch, to the trunk, or — for shrubs — almost to the ground.

Heading back results in a shorter branch with more growth just below the cut. Thinning lets light and air into the interior of a plant but does not change its size or natural form.

SEE ALSO: *Heading Back, page 61, and Thinning Fruit, page 235.*

Q How do I make a proper pruning cut, and how should it look when it's done?

A Much of the skill in pruning involves knowing how to make good use of buds in order to redirect growth or rejuvenate the plant.

When pruning, make your cuts above a promising bud or side branch, to a main branch, or at the ground. Make a slanting cut about ¼ inch above a bud. In addition to being the best spot to stimulate new growth in the bud below, it leaves fewer stubs, and the slant dries out faster after a rain.

Avoid pruning too close to the bud. The tender part of the bud will be too near the cut, may not receive enough sap, and will dry out — or freezing temperatures may damage it. If you prune too far from the bud, the dead stub will rot and look ugly, and the rot can spread easily to the rest of the tree. Likewise, when you're cutting off dead branches, always cut back to a live bud or branch so that no dead wood will be left on the plant. Don't make a flat-topped cut. This cut is not only stubby and unattractive, but it is also slow to dry out after a rain, inviting rot and disease.

INCORRECT CUTS

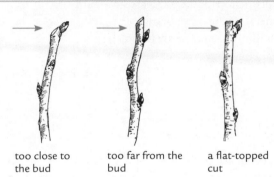

too close to
the bud

too far from the
bud

a flat-topped
cut

CORRECT METHOD

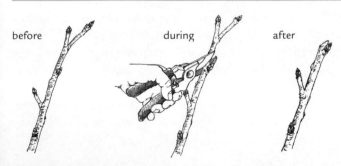

before

during

after

Q Where should I cut when two branches intersect?

A If you're removing the terminal (upper or outermost) shoot on a branch, then cut back (head back) to ¼ inch above a side branch that is growing in the direction in which you want the plant to grow. For best results, prune to a branch at least one-third the diameter of the main branch or trunk. This will minimize new growth on the same branch.

heading back to
a smaller branch

Q I see lots of buds on a branch. How do I know which buds to keep and which to cut? Where's the best place to make a basic pruning cut?

A If you're pruning a spreading and upward-growing tree and want to avoid crossed or inward-heading branches, look for an outside bud and cut just above it. A limb or twig growing from an outside bud tends to grow outward and upward; a branch from an inside bud tends to grow inward. Pruning branches to inside buds will lead to ingrown limbs. Cutting above outside buds produces a more spreading tree. (Dotted lines in the illustrations at right show future growth if colored limbs are removed.)

Most deciduous trees and shrubs have alternate buds: when you see a bud on one side of the branch, usually you will find one farther along on the other side. A few trees, however, such as maples and ashes, grow their buds and leaves directly opposite each other. When you're pruning a branch with opposite buds, cut just above one of these double buds and snip or rub off the inside bud, leaving only the outside bud intact.

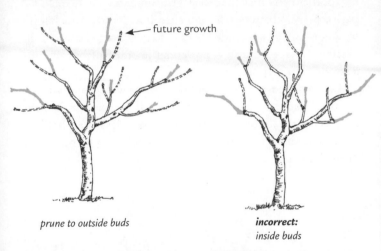

prune to outside buds

incorrect:
inside buds

TIMELY TIP

Late winter or early spring is usually a good time to prune: you can see buds easily before foliage hides them.

Q What is a weak crotch?

A When a branch has a weak crotch, it typically joins the trunk at an acute angle (less that 45 degrees) and has bark lodged in the crotch (included bark) between the branch and trunk or between two stems of equal size competing to be the tree's leader (codominant stems). Trees with branches too big for the trunk may have weak attachments. Where included bark is present between the branches, it won't take much force to split off a limb. Included bark — bark squeezed deep in the narrow V-shaped union — prevents the branch from making a strong connection.

Conversely, strong crotches tend to be wider and with no included bark. A bark ridge may form in the crotch, and the limb is clearly subordinate to the trunk — less than half the trunk's diameter — allowing a branch collar to form at base of the limb.

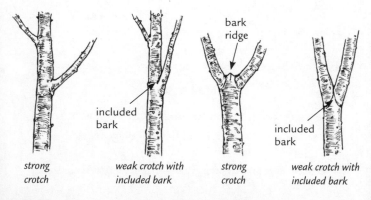

strong crotch *weak crotch with included bark* *strong crotch* *weak crotch with included bark*

Pinching

Q Some of my shrubs produce such soft new growth that using clippers on them seems like overkill. Can I prune the soft stems with my hands?

A Some woody plants produce soft new growth that you can pinch off by hand. By removing a terminal bud or a wayward lateral bud with your thumb and forefinger, you'll temporarily stop all growth in that area. Many gardeners prune by pinching off any new growth that is heading in the wrong direction. For harder stems too advanced for hand pinching, some gardeners like to carry a sharp knife or a pair of pruners on their belt, ready to draw them out at the first sign of unwanted growth.

Q When can I pinch back woody plants?

A Spring and summer, when plants are actively growing. With dedicated, frequent pinching throughout the growing season, you can efficiently remove suckers, shorten branch growth, take off extra tops, and redirect growth with the least possible shock to the plant. It is also a useful way to disbud

pinching

flowers and thin out fruit. Strolling frequently through the yard or orchard during the growing season, pinching as you go, is an excellent, low-tech way to prevent future trouble.

Unkind Cuts

Q I cut the deciduous shrubs below my windows to the same height each year. Now the tops look green but the bottoms are brown. Why?

A The pruning technique you used is called heading. This type of cut occurs between growth nodes where buds and leaves are attached. The result is a cluster of shoots right below the cut. Such thick growth occurs on top that it can block sunlight from reaching the plant's interior, which eventually dies off. For a more natural, fuller look and more foliage from top to bottom, cut small branches to various heights and make these cuts to an outside bud or branch.

Q My neighbor wants me to top my old Scotch pines to preserve her view of the bay. Should I do it?

A NO. Topping mature trees — also known as tipping, hatracking, heading, beheading, or dehorning — is common but some consider it a crime against nature. Beheading a big tree, or cutting back its lead stem between two adjacent nodes, ruins its shape and can harm and eventually kill it. On old fruit trees, even if production improves for a couple of years after topping, it ultimately wounds the tree. Rot, cracking, weakening, and breakage can result from topping, making a tree susceptible to pests and diseases and potentially dangerous to people and buildings nearby.

Trees have the wonderful habit of growing each year whether or not you pay much attention to them. Suddenly you notice that they are reaching into utility lines or blocking a choice view. Though you want to spare your utility lines and preserve your view, you must resist the temptation to cut off their tops.

So what can you do to avoid topping? Don't plant trees bigger than the space you have, and don't plant a tall tree where a short one is called for. Avoid growing trees under power lines, unless you choose trees that mature at no more than 25 feet high.

Shearing

Q The house I bought has an overgrown evergreen hedge. How can I prune it into shape?

A Shearing is a type of pruning that works well on formal hedges that would take too long to trim back stem by stem. This technique removes some of a plant's vegetation from its surface by cutting it with a sharp instrument — usually pruning shears or an electric hedge clipper. The softness of this growth makes the work comparatively easy. When you're finished, the newly cut ends will heal over, form a bud at the end, and be ready to grow the following spring. Shearing works best if you train sheared hedges from their first year and maintain them consistently.

Shearing works well when you want to give your plants a geometrical look. Some gardeners shear individual evergreens into different shapes like cubes and globes. A sheared globe, for example, can make an interesting garden accent . . . or it can look like a meatball in a foundation planting.

A common mistake in shearing hedges is to wait until the end of the growing season. If a plant has its new growth neatly chopped off late each year, few buds will have a chance to get started and it will never get bushier. Plus, no new growth will appear to cover the clipped ends, so they'll remain exposed throughout the year. Shearing back into bare wood can kill branches of some conifers; others will sprout new growth. Consult the Plant-by-Plant Pruning Guide, starting on page 311, for advice about your particular plants.

shear to shape and control

Q When should I shear?

A In general, shear after plant growth starts in late spring. This way, redirecting will begin early enough to be effective. The growth of the end buds will be curtailed immediately and new buds will eventually form where the cuts were made. But even before that, the dormant buds will be stimulated to grow, resulting in a bushier plant or a tighter hedge.

Heading Back (Lateral Pruning)

Q Where's the right place on a branch to make a pruning cut?

A Cut back to a lateral (side) branch. This is called heading back or lateral pruning. The lateral you choose depends upon the size of the branch and the desired effect of the cut. If the diameter of the lateral branch is at least one-third the diameter of the pruned branch, you can prevent the thick sprouting that occurs with heading back. In this case, the side branch is sizable enough to suppress the hormone that lets dormant lateral buds develop (apical dominance).

Q I have an old red maple shading the west side of my house. A big low branch is touching the clapboards. How can I get rid of that branch without damaging the tree or my house?

A For the safety of your home, you may have to cut some large limbs from older shade trees and fruit trees. Just as you cut to a live bud on small trees and shrubs, cut back large limbs to a live branch or the main trunk. Large, heavy tree limbs need removal in stages (see below) to avoid breaking and splitting the next branch or trunk under the weight of the partial cut. For best results, follow these steps:

1. Make an undercut with the saw about 6 inches out from the trunk.

2. About 1 inch beyond the first cut, saw off the limb. Don't bear down on the saw — let the sharp teeth do the cutting.

3. Cut off the remaining stub. Cut to the outside edge of the enlarged collar, where a limb joins a larger limb or the trunk. Cutting to the branch collar enables the tree to seal off the wounded area.

correct: cut to branch collar

wrong: flush cut

Q Should I dress pruning cuts with tree paint?

A It used to be the custom to paint over pruning cuts or seal them with a tree dressing, but expert horticulturists and foresters now agree that these products do more harm than good. A tree seals off wounded areas and starts the healing process by itself.

Thinning

Q We have a tulip tree at the foot of our driveway near the house. Over the years it's dropped several branches in high winds. How can I stop this?

A The tulip tree (*Liriodendron tulipifera*) is a fast grower with brittle wood and a dense crown of big leaves, which act like a sail in high winds. Wind pushes rather than penetrates the canopy. Limbs, particularly those with weak branch attachments, may break under the pressure. Thinning the crown reduces its mass and helps the tree withstand the effects of wind and weather. Thinning a tree or shrub also lets light into its interior and increases air circulation.

An arborist can remove dead and diseased branches from the canopy, cutting back to a lateral branch or to the trunk. Later, branches that are crossed or rub against each other can come off. If suckers are growing on or at the base of the trunk, those can come off too. Remove poorly attached branches, since they are most in danger of breaking in powerful gusts of wind or under the weight of ice and snow. It's best to prune sparingly and space this pruning over a period of several years.

SEE ALSO: *Thinning Fruit, page 235.*

Limbing Up

 What is limbing up?

It's the ideal way to shape a shade tree. Just clip off all limbs that start close to the ground, thereby directing more of the tree's growth upward. Limbing up is also called basal pruning. Sometimes it's called lifting the crown or raising the canopy, though the height of the tree doesn't change.

Removing lower limbs not only makes a tree look more "treelike," but it also lets in additional light and air to make your lawn, flowers, and other plants grow better. It can make your house more comfortable and energy efficient year-round. Large deciduous trees are nature's air conditioners. They provide cooling shade in summer, and after their leaves have fallen in autumn, sunlight can enter your house for warmth when you need it most. A few seasons of noting how the sun enters your house at different times of the year will help you to ascertain how many lower limbs to remove to let in light.

Q Some big trees in my yard block the view of my neighbor's driveway, but I've been told I should remove the lower branches. Is that necessary?

A If your tree is part of a screen, you probably won't want to prune off lower branches. If you want to picnic, play, and easily mow under the trees, limbing up is a good idea.

limbing up

Q My pine tree has grown so large I don't know what to do with it. I don't want to cut it down because it was a gift from my parents. What can I do?

A Removing a few low branches will help bring the rest of your plants into view. By limbing up this spreading evergreen (see below), the area under the tree opens up to provide a view and access to the lower-growing plantings beyond. The technique can also show off beautiful bark, bring more light onto your property, and help control trunk-boring insects. Most conifers look better branched to the ground, and only the dead, shaded out, basal limbs should be removed.

before pruning   after pruning

TIPS FOR SUCCESSFUL LIMBING UP

Spread out heavy pruning over several years. If a tree needs more than a couple of branches removed, wait two or three years before you attempt the next pruning.

Remove dead and damaged limbs at any time. The lower limbs of evergreens are often dead or nearly so, especially if the trees are growing close together. These can be cut off in any season without damage to the tree.

Always cut back a large limb to the branch collar, so that no stub is left to rot. Leave the collar (see page 63), which speeds healing.

Q When can I begin removing lower limbs?

A Start when a tree is 12 to 16 feet tall. Don't procrastinate. Not only is it easier to cut off the bottom limbs of the tree when it is still small, but you also leave smaller pruning wounds to heal over.

As the tree grows larger and wider, these limbs spread outward and downward. Unless you remove them, they can become a nuisance by the time the tree is 15 or 20 years old, particularly on trees planted by streets and walkways.

PRUNING PRACTICES RIGHT AND WRONG

Q How far up should I remove branches when limbing up?

A A distance of 8 feet from the ground to the first branches is good for most large trees if you want to walk or drive under them. You can also limb up a small tree. Whatever a tree's height, at least the top two-thirds should be canopy. Plant firs and other pyramidal evergreens that keep their lower limbs where they won't need to be limbed up.

Root Pruning

Q My neighbor says that I should do "root pruning" when moving shrubs around my property. What does he mean?

A Root pruning is less understood and thus less practiced than any other type of pruning. Many gardeners will have no part of it. They consider the roots of a plant sacred and not to be disturbed.

Nurseries often cut a circle around field-growing trees and shrubs every year or two to encourage a compact yet full root system and reduce shock or setback when transplanting. To move trees or shrubs in your own yard or to dig up wild specimens (with permission), use a similar method and root-prune them one season before moving them. Do this on small trees or shrubs, and leave the pruning and moving of large trees to professionals.

The theory behind root pruning is that fine new roots will form at cuts on a recently root-pruned woody plant. Best outcomes occur with small, robust, deciduous shrubs and vines, but you can also root-prune evergreens and trees. Cutting the roots of old, weak plants can be deadly.

Shallow-rooted plants — those with many small roots in the top 8 inches of soil — transplant better than those with taproots, such as young white oaks and pines. For large or valuable trees, hire a professional arborist to do the job.

GOOD REASONS FOR ROOT PRUNING

Use this valuable skill for any number of tasks:

- ◆ To control plant size
- ◆ To increase new roots before transplanting
- ◆ To get young trees and shrubs off to a good start
- ◆ To slow growth
- ◆ To force reluctant flowering trees and shrubs to bloom
- ◆ To persuade slow-to-start fruit trees to begin bearing
- ◆ To keep container plants from outgrowing their pots

Q I grow a potted bay laurel, which I bring indoors for the winter. I want to keep it in the same container, but it's grown awfully big. What can I do?

A Root pruning, a technique common in bonsai growing, is essential for container plants such as bay laurel, evergreens growing in pots, and citrus because it can control their growth. Most houses and gardens don't have room enough for gardeners to keep repotting their plants indefinitely into larger containers. If your bay laurel is becoming unwieldy, remove it from its pot, cut back all outside roots, and replant it with some new soil in the same pot.

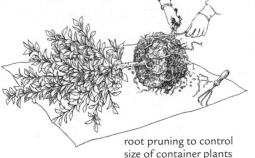

root pruning to control size of container plants

Q How do I root-prune a shrub before transplanting it?

A To root-prune a shrub, cut straight down around the plant's root zone with a sharp spade. To determine the size of the pruning circle, you'll first need to figure out the size of the root-ball you'll be transplanting. Measure the diameter of the shrub and multiply it by two-thirds. That number will give you the approximate size of the root-ball you'll be digging up: If the shrub to be transplanted measures 3 feet across, the root-ball will be 2 feet across. Prune roots about 6 inches in from the edge of the root-ball. In the case of the 3-foot shrub, that would mean root pruning a circle about 1½ feet wide. Remember that most of the feeder roots are in the top 8 inches of soil and that the key to successful establishment is proper planting and keeping the soil consistently moist, not too wet or too dry, through regular deep watering. The directions below are for a shade tree with a 2-inch trunk.

1. In early spring, before bud break, use a sharp, long-bladed spade to make a downward vertical cut through the soil about 2 feet from the trunk. Some big roots may be tough, and a firm thrust will be necessary to sever them. When digging a young evergreen, cut the circle at the outer spread of the branches. New roots will then grow within the circle, resulting in a tight root-ball safe to move without excess stress to the plant.

root pruning

2. That same year in fall, right after leaf drop, dig a hole where you want to set the tree or shrub. Then cut another circle completely around the tree that is slightly outside the one where you had previously pruned the roots. This will ensure that you include all the new roots in the root-ball. Dig and transplant the tree to the new location, keeping the root-ball intact. Plant immediately, following the usual directions for planting.

dig root-ball outside root-pruning cuts

Q When should I root-prune?

A The best time is about two months before you transplant, so that new roots grow at the root cuts but don't spread far beyond the root-ball. Traditionalists root-prune in March before new growth begins for fall transplanting or in October/November after leaf drop for spring transplanting.

Q I'm going to the nursery to purchase a bunch of flowering shrubs to plant around my new house. Do they need pruning at planting?

A Shrubs that will eventually grow 6 feet tall or more, such as lilacs and viburnums, should be treated as trees when you plant them. Balled-and-burlapped and container-grown shrubs usually need little pruning at planting. Cut out damaged branches. Leave other branches intact to encourage upward growth and earlier blooming.

Q I just brought home a young rhododendron from the nursery. Should I prune it now?

A It may not need any pruning now. Still, it's a good idea to check the condition of the root mass and do whatever is needed to correct it:

1. Tip the root-ball out of the pot. Check the outside roots. Some trees that have been growing for several years in a large container before being sold will develop a circular habit of root growth.

remove pot

If this pattern continues after a tree is planted, the increasing size of the encircling roots can strangle it in later years.

2. Cut back encircling roots with a sharp, stout knife or clip them with hand pruners, and lightly trim the bottom of the root-ball. If roots are fine and dense, make three or four

make shallow slices

73

shallow slices through them with a sharp knife. Don't worry about harming the plant; you are actually doing it a favor by helping it to grow more freely.

3. Gently comb the remaining tangle of roots with your fingers. This encourages quick growth of new, outward-reaching roots. Now you're ready to plant.

untangle the root-ball

Q I ordered some bare-root shrubs online. Do they need special attention when they arrive?

A The care you take now will ensure a great start and a promising future in your garden. Begin by inspecting the roots to determine if they were damaged when the plant was dug up. Broken, ragged ends should be cut off cleanly so that they will heal over quickly and begin to send out the hair roots that supply food to the plant. An overlong root may need shortening to make the plant more convenient to handle.

Be sure to keep the roots in a tub of water when you inspect them because they will suffer badly if they are exposed to the air for more than a few minutes. (Newly acquired, bare-root nursery stock should always be soaked for 5 or 6 hours after you get it home.) Follow the steps below when pruning a newly planted, bareroot shrub:

1. If any roots are broken, use hand pruners to cut them so there will be a minimum amount of wound to heal over. Leave other roots intact.
2. Remove dead, damaged, rubbing, and overcrowded branches, but no more than one-third of its growth; the shrub needs enough leaves to sustain the plant. Always remember to cut on a slant above an outside bud. (See page 52.)

remove dead or damaged roots and branches

Q Will root pruning slow the top growth of my tree?

A An established tree is sometimes root-pruned, even if it will never be transplanted, in order to slow down its growth. Although you may think it more logical to check tree growth by cutting back the branches, this way isn't always best. Pruned trees usually try to regrow branches to replace those they've lost as soon as possible, so a tree may grow faster than ever. Root pruning, on the other hand, cuts off part of the supply of nutrients and thus slows growth.

In addition to controlling tree size, you may want to slow down top growth for other reasons. Trees or shrubs grown in decorative containers may need their roots pruned to keep the roots from growing too long and girdling the root-ball. Fruit trees in rich soil often do so well that they go right on growing for many years without producing any fruit. Sometimes flowering trees will also make lush growth for a long time but won't bloom. Root pruning can slow down a tree's growth activity and force it to bloom and bear. Bonsai growers rely heavily on root and branch pruning to keep their plants small yet ancient looking.

CHAPTER 5

Pruning Deciduous Shade Trees

A shade tree is a lifetime project, so choose a location where it can grow to its majestic stature without heavy pruning. Don't take the term *shade tree* literally, because it embraces trees like the Lombardy poplar, which actually offers little in the way of shade. Shade trees can (1) define borders, (2) shield a house from noisy highways, (3) provide a protected living or playing area, and (4) offer autumn color, among many other practical and aesthetic purposes. Because large trees are the kings and queens of the landscape, you should place them with care to avoid the need for heavy pruning.

Q Just what is a shade tree?

A The term *shade tree* usually connotes a deciduous tree, although evergreens can also be shade trees. Some evergreen trees are shade trees, as discussed in chapter 7.

Planting Trees

Q Can I plant my new tree as it is from the nursery or must I do something to it first?

A The answer to your question depends upon the tree's packaging and condition at purchase. When you buy a plant, its roots may have been dug with a tight ball of earth and wrapped in burlap or plastic, it may be growing in a pot of soil, or the bare roots may be surrounded only with moist moss. Each kind of packaging requires different care at planting time.

Q How do I plant a balled-and-burlapped tree?

A If your new tree comes with its roots enclosed in a large ball of soil, you probably don't need to prune much at planting time, except for cutting back a few extra-long or damaged roots emerging from the root-ball. Just be careful not to damage the root-ball as you maneuver it to the hole.

How do I plant a bare-root tree?

If you purchase a small bare-root tree or dig one up in a friend's yard and transplant it, you should cut off broken roots and damaged branches when you plant. Remember to make your cuts on a slant, just above a bud, and cut to an outside bud on the side branches. Follow these simple guidelines:

1. Prune off any broken roots with a smooth cut.
2. Start pruning for a strong structure during the next dormant season. Remove any damaged wood, leaving a central leader and as much leaf space as possible.

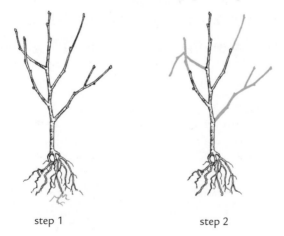

step 1   step 2

Q How do I plant a container-grown tree?

A The roots of some trees that have been growing for several years in a large container before being sold may circle the outside of the root-ball. If this pattern continues after the tree is planted, the increasing size of the encircling roots can actually strangle the tree in later years. Check the outside roots to see if this strangulation is occurring. If it is, spread out the offending roots or prune back woody girdling roots and plant the tree in a wide, shallow hole.

Training Shade Trees

Q We lost trees from ice and wind damage last winter. Is there any way we can protect the trees we plant as replacements?

A First, choose the right tree. The trees at a reputable retail nursery should be well on their way to a healthy, strong form thanks to early formative pruning, so there's not much for you to do. Still, young trees may need occasional pruning to develop a sturdy structure. Trees grown with a single leader are more likely to have a strong trunk and sturdy permanent (scaffold) branches that can withstand harsh weather. Trees with multiple leaders usually have narrow crotches with included bark, which makes limbs more susceptible to ice and wind damage. Training means pruning out weak branches in favor of strong ones over time.

Q How can I train my young shade tree to have a strong form?

A To give your tree the strongest form, train it to a central leader with well-attached branches (scaffolds). The following tips are for training central-leader trees, not trees intentionally grown with multiple trunks.

1. The tree should have a central vertical branch or leader growing above the other branches. You will need to deal with competing leaders — vigorous vertical side branches or secondary trunks nearing the height of the central leader — by shortening the side branches and removing the secondary trunks.

2. Remove weak, crossing, and rubbing branches. Crossing branches create congestion in the tree crown and block sunlight from reaching the limbs. Rubbing wears away the bark, giving pathogens easy entry.

3. No two branches should emerge at the same spot on the trunk.

4. Healthy scaffold branches — the main branches forming the framework of the tree — emerge at different heights and in different locations around the trunk, like spokes on a wheel when seen from a bird's-eye view. In a large shade tree, the

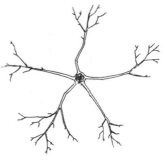

healthy scaffold branches

scaffold branches should typically be 12 to 18 inches apart on the trunk.

5. The angle between a branch and the trunk is normally strongest between 45 and 90 degrees. Remove branches and multiple trunks growing at acute angles to the main trunk.

6. Over time, remove any bottom branches that would grow so long and heavy that they could break.

Q How long does it take for a tree to develop a strong form?

A Structural pruning takes place during a tree's first 25 or so years. Ideally, remove problem branches when they're young and measure less than one-third the diameter of the trunk.

a strong central-leader form

Maintaining Shade Trees

Q We have a gorgeous shade tree in the front yard. It's about 10 years old. We've never done a thing to it. Should we prune it?

A If your tree grows well, significant pruning may not be needed for many years. There are times, however, when you should intervene: Remember the old saying that an ounce of prevention is worth a pound of cure.

PROBLEM 1. Crossed branches develop or the top begins to grow crooked.

SOLUTION. Do some snipping and pinching during the growing season. Wait until the dormant season to do the heavier pruning.

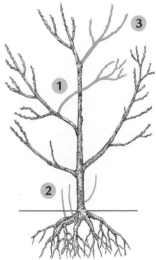

PROBLEM 2. Abundant sucker growth appears from the base of the tree.

SOLUTION. Use a saw or loppers to cut off the suckers, and any weak lower limbs, close to the trunk.

PROBLEM 3. Your tree develops a competing leader.

SOLUTION. Cut out any competing leaders that develop.

Q When's the best time to remove a large limb?

A Pruning in late winter or early spring before a tree leafs out may be less stressful for the tree. Also, at this time you can see the structure of a deciduous tree.

Q My oak tree has ugly growths on some of the twigs. What are they, and what can I do about them?

A These abnormal tissue growths are called galls. Leaf, twig, and stem galls look bad but won't do permanent harm to a tree. Prune out ugly twigs in light infestations, which can be caused by insects such as mites, wasps, aphids, and midge flies. Oaks are particularly susceptible to galls.

WHEN GALLS ARE NOT HARMLESS

Crown galls, caused by a bacterium, are different from the common leaf and stem galls, which are caused by insects. Crown galls form at the soil line on the principal tree roots (and sometimes on lesser roots) or higher on the trunk and branches. Among affected plants are fruit trees such as apple and cherry, nut trees, and shrubs like roses, raspberries, blackberries, and burning bush — about 140 plant genera in all. These galls start out tan, smooth, and spongy but turn hard, rough, and black with age. Effects of this disease range from stunted growth to plant death. The bacterium can enter the plant through grafting or pruning wounds, so when disease is present, it's crucial to keep tools clean by sterilizing after each cut. First, clean dirt off tools, then dip them in a household disinfectant such as Lysol or rubbing alcohol. Wipe off excess disinfectant before making the next cut.

Pruning Older Shade Trees

Q Some old trees on my property are in pretty bad shape. Should I take their age into account when I'm pruning them?

A Yes, because trees, like animals and humans, go through various life stages, from infancy to old age. Sooner or later, each tree will reach a stage when it is impractical to spend vast amounts of time and money on it, and you must consider replacement. It may be difficult to make the decision to recycle an old tree as firewood and mulch, but this process is also a part of good gardening and conservation. Old, derelict trees are not only unsightly, but they are also dangerous and harbor insects and disease. Consider these guidelines.

1. When a tree or shrub is young, do corrective pruning: Pinch buds and redirect branches to persuade the plant to grow in a strong, attractive shape.

2. During the prime of its life, a tree or shrub may benefit from corrective pruning and pruning for rejuvenation, production, balance, or usefulness.

3. In a tree's old age, prune mainly to keep it healthy and prolong its useful life. No amount of pruning can prolong the life of a Lombardy poplar much beyond its anticipated 20 or 30 years, but a bristlecone pine may live for thousands of years without removing a branch. Find out the approximate life span of each plant in order to prune it properly.

4. Adjust your pruning to the plant's present state of vitality, which varies by age and species, and from year

to year depending on soil and weather. Just because a flowering crab apple may thrive from a severe cutback when it is four years old doesn't mean that it can stand the same treatment at age 40.

Q Can I do structural pruning on old trees?

A If you neglect to do early shaping of a tree and large limbs grow low on the trunk, be sure that the plant has a healthy crown before cutting off any basal branches. Never cut off more than a quarter of the crown or branch area (10 to 15 percent is better) in a year, because leaves are necessary to nourish the tree. You could probably prune a tree 30 feet tall with 25 feet of limb growth 5 feet up from the base of the crown in any one year without endangering the tree.

If several good-sized limbs must be cut off, spread the project over a few years by cutting off only one or two each fall or every other fall. This way, you give the tree time to grow additional leaf mass at the top to compensate for the loss of basal limbs, and you avoid shocking the tree.

Q How can I know whether an old tree that needs lots of work is worth saving?

A If you own a decrepit tree, or if you acquired a sad specimen along with your new home, you should consider if it is worth saving before you spend lots of money to save it.

Weather, disease, and insects take their toll, no matter how carefully you plan a tree's location or perform its initial shaping, and life span varies greatly according to species. Some giant sequoias (*Sequoiadendron giganteum*) are about 3,500 years old, and trees of many other species in this country are older than the republic. However, some poplar and cherry trees are over the hill by the time they reach the age of 30. Check with your Cooperative Extension Service or consult a certified arborist for information about your specific type of tree.

If your mature cherry tree (*Prunus* spp.) has an isolated problem, such as a black knot–infested limb, remove it. It's important to cut carefully, so that you do as little damage as possible to the tree and the surrounding plants and structures. Arborists tie a rope around a limb before cutting it. They make large cuts, as shown on page 62, then ease the limb gently to the ground.

remove diseased limb

tie rope to a limb
before cutting

Q I'm worried because a major branch on my Bradford pear tree started splitting off. What can I do to stop it?

A If the tree is old and the crack is deep, get rid of the tree; it's a danger to people and property. If the tree is young and has two leaders — a likely cause of splitting and cracking — prune one off. For short-lived varieties with naturally poor branching habits like Bradford pear, cables or bolts are not usually recommended.

However, professional arborists may use bracing to secure a heavy, weak, stressed, or splitting limb on other trees. This involves drilling holes through the trunk and limb, and installing cables and/or bolts to provide extra strength. Before pruning or removing a tree, consult with an arborist to see if cabling or bracing can save it.

Q My tree has a big cavity in it. Should I clean it out and fill it?

A Although older trees are most apt to develop big cavities, trees of any age may develop openings or cavities as a result of wood-decay fungi. These hollows make habitats for many bird and small mammal species, and filling them takes away that habitat. In fact, caring for trees differs from caring for your teeth. Although filling a festering tooth helps stabilize the tooth and prevent further decay, filling a tree cavity with cement makes the surrounding wood rot faster. If you're displeased with the appearance of a hollow, an arborist can fill the cavity with special tree foam that does not affect the tree's natural movements. An arborist also uses braces and cables to stabilize trees. If your tree cannot be stabilized and endangers people or property, you must remove it.

SAFETY REMINDER

Never prune near electrical or utility wires. Contact your city, town, or utility company to do the job.

Q Big beautiful trees grow around my home. Should I hire someone to prune them or can I prune them myself?

A Tree work can be dangerous, particularly when it involves big, mature trees. Tree climbing and pruning high or heavy branches are dangerous tasks that require skill, time, and training to learn. Trained arborists treat trees with respect. When they use a ladder, they protect the tree by not sliding the ladder along the branches, which would scar the bark. Professionals use a rope to lower pruned limbs and avoid letting them crash into other limbs, people, and property.

For big trees, hire an arborist with credentials from state and national organizations such as the American Society of Consulting Arborists (ASCA), the International Society of Arboriculture (ISA), and the Tree Care Industry Association (TCIA) to do the work. Before hiring an arborist or tree specialist, check the company's proof of insurance to avoid liability for an accident on your property.

CHAPTER 6

Pruning Flowering Trees and Ornamental Shrubs

Want your flowering trees and shrubs to look their best each year? That's every gardener's goal. In this chapter, you'll learn about pruning your favorites, including lilac, forsythia, viburnum, and hydrangea. For information on rhododendrons and other evergreen bloomers, check the section on broadleaf evergreens in chapter 7.

Flowering Trees

Q How can I train my Japanese tree lilac to stay strong and healthy and look its best?

A Some plants, such as Japanese tree lilac (*Syringa reticulata*) and mountain ash (*Sorbus* spp.), form a lot of lower limbs. Remove these for a more treelike effect, especially until the specimen is mature. As a rule, the branches on most ornamental flowering trees are not heavy, and their berries and fruit seldom add much weight, so careful training of the limb structure is not as necessary as it is on fruit trees.

A properly pruned flowering tree will be strong and less likely to break in wind- and ice storms. Flowering crab apples can live for over a century and tree lilacs for even longer. The key is to train the tree to grow with a central leader for the first 10 feet at least. In other words, train a flowering tree as a tree rather than as a large bush.

Q What should I keep in mind when I prune my flowering trees?

A Follow these guidelines to keep flowering trees attractive and healthy:

◆ Keep the tree trunk as a single stem. Don't allow groups of heavy branches to grow from the lower part of the tree.

◆ Remove all suckers that sprout from the roots. Grafted trees such as flowering crab apples and hawthorns may send up a lot of suckers from the rootstock. Cut them off immediately, because they grow so fast that they can quickly overtake and crowd out the desirable part of the tree.

◆ Prune back branches that upset the symmetry and appearance of the tree.

◆ Remove all branches growing close to the ground. They interfere with lawn mowing and are unattractive.

◆ Thin. As the tree gets older, take out branches growing too densely or crossing others, so the remaining ones continue to bloom well. Remember, thinning enables air to move and light to penetrate the crown. Avoid overpruning.

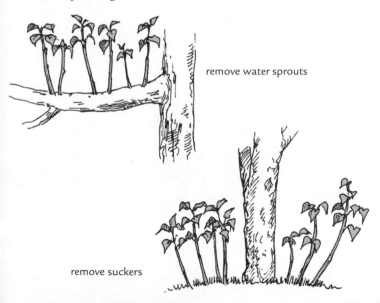

remove water sprouts

remove suckers

Q It's not spring until my flowering crab apple comes into bloom. I know it needs some tidying up. How can I do that without changing its natural form?

A Follow these steps, consulting the drawing below:

1. Cut off all suckers.
2. Prune branches that upset the tree's symmetry.
3. Remove low-growing branches.
4. Thin out crossed and densely growing branches.

The result is a graceful, airy tree, which is not only attractive, but also healthy.

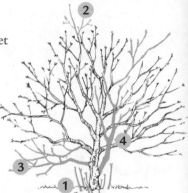

before pruning

after pruning

Q What's the best time to prune my flowering cherries?

A For maximum bloom, prune them just after the blossoms fade. Prune trees that produce attractive berries or fruit in late winter so you won't interfere with the display.

Q Is it worth my time to restore an old flowering tree that used to be pretty but now looks kind of sad?

A The answer depends on the variety of plant, its vigor, the care with which you prune, and your climate. You can slash back some tropical and semitropical plants mercilessly and they will quickly grow back into youthful, handsome plants. Trees and shrubs in northern climates need to be treated more carefully, and in most cases it's best to spread out major pruning jobs over several years.

Cut back only a few limbs at a time, and as they regrow, you can remove a few more. In this way, you can revitalize your tree. Gradual renewal is better for the plant's health, and its appearance is less drastically altered in the process. Late winter or early spring is usually the best time for such restorative pruning. The plant will be entering its period of most vigorous growth and thus be more resilient.

Keep in mind that flowering shrubs and trees have definite life spans, and if they are nearing the end of their days, pruning won't help them revive. Just as with fruit and shade trees that reach this stage, it is better to cut them down and plant new ones nearby.

Deciduous Ornamental Shrubs

Q Do I need to prune my flowering shrubs?

A Many shrubs rarely need pruning, except to remove dead or damaged branches. Sometimes, however, you must remove old wood to rejuvenate them, thin wood growing too thickly, and keep suckers under control. Some shrubs, such as bush honeysuckle, viburnum, and lilac, may grow too tall for their location and need heading back. A few, including many forsythias, produce dense thickets of branches; annual thinning can reduce the number of dead or straggly twigs in spring.

Q I'm confused. When do I prune my flowering shrubs?

A Prune shrubs that form flowers on new wood (grown the same season) in late fall, late winter, or early spring before the buds show green and not when they are actively growing. The best time to prune a flowering shrub that blooms on old wood (at least one year old) is just after the blossoms have faded, before it grows new branches and forms the buds that will bloom the next year.

Late winter is the best time to prune the shrubs that are grown mostly for their foliage (Japanese maple) or those grown primarily for the beauty of their winter bark (redtwig dogwood). Remove broken, dead, rubbing, or diseased branches whenever you notice them.

SEE ALSO: *Plant-by-Plant Pruning Guide, starting on page 311.*

PRUNING TIMES

Some shrubs to prune when dormant (before bloom)

Beautyberry (*Callicarpa* spp.)

Bluebeard (*Caryopteris* × *clandonensis*)

Bottlebrush buckeye (*Aesculus parviflora*)

Bush clover (*Lespedeza thunbergii*)

Butterfly bush (*Buddleia davidii*)

Crape myrtle (*Lagerstroemia indica*)

Red chokeberry (*Aronia arbutifolia*)

Rose of Sharon (*Hibiscus syriacus*)

Southern bush honeysuckle (*Diervilla sessilifolia*)

Summersweet (*Clethra* spp.)

Some shrubs to prune after bloom

Azalea (*Rhododendron* spp.)

Beauty bush (*Kolkwitzia amabilis*)

Broom (*Cytisus* spp.)

Deutzia (*Deutzia* spp.)

Forsythia (*Forsythia* spp.)

Fothergilla (*Fothergilla* spp.)

Mock orange (*Philadelphus coronarius*)

Rhododendron (*Rhododendron* spp.)

Viburnum (*Viburnum* spp.)

Virginia sweetspire (*Itea virginica*)

Weigela (*Weigela* spp.)

Witch hazel (*Hamamelis* spp.)

Q My summersweets are starting to look big and messy. How do I get them back in shape?

A Summersweet (*Clethra alnifolia*) blooms on new wood. It can spread by suckers and look unbalanced over time. If you prune it lightly in late winter or early spring, you can avoid drastic pruning later on. Just remove excess suckers, damaged branches, and some of the oldest, longest shoots by cutting them off at the base; that promotes new growth from the ground without sacrificing any flowers.

If you grow shrubs that bloom on old wood, such as glossy abelia, Japanese kerria, and viburnums, you can use the same method to keep them groomed, waiting until right after blooming to prune them in order to preserve the current season's blooms.

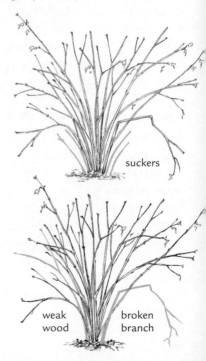

suckers

weak wood

broken branch

Check the plant-by-plant guide (page 311) to determine whether your shrub blooms on old or new wood. Then follow these steps when pruning:

1. Remove all suckers.
2. Remove dead, broken, and weak wood.

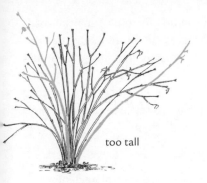

too tall

the result

3. Remove some older, taller branches.
4. The result — a neater, healthier shrub.

Q I love lilacs. When should I prune them? Do they bloom on old or new wood?

A Lilac (*Syringa* spp.) is one of the most widely planted and beloved flowering shrubs in the country. Lilacs were introduced into the colonies so long ago that some bushes growing in American yards are more than 200 years old. Enjoy the sweet scent of lilacs, which bloom on old wood, and delay pruning until right after they bloom.

remove faded flowers

After the shrub blooms, cut off the spent flowers (deadhead). Remove fading blooms only; don't touch the stems and leaves. Clip just above the buds forming for next year's blooms. The farther you cut back, the more likely that you are picking off next year's blooms. By pruning off the old blossoms, you help to ensure regular blooming. Of course, if you have a long hedge of tall-growing bushes, this snipping may be impractical and you'll have to settle for heavy blooms whenever the lilacs want to provide them.

Q We just bought an old farm with several ancient, straggly, but super-fragrant lilacs growing by the house. How should I prune them?

A Because lilacs are such long-lived plants, often they are long overdue for attention. Neglected, elderly bushes need careful pruning with both clippers and a saw.

Follow these steps when renewing lilacs and other old shrubs in early spring:

1. Select several of the strong, younger trunks to remain. These will become your new bush. Cut off all the rest (those shaded in drawing), especially old and decrepit ones — these have lost most of their vitality anyway. Make all cuts close to the ground, and cut carefully so that you don't slash into any adjoining stems. The exact number of trunks you leave will depend on the area your bush covers and whether you want to shrink its size.

2. Cut away the small, thick sucker growth at the plant's base. These stems crowd both the main bush and each other. Removing them will let you see which of the larger stems (shaded in drawing) still need to be cut.

3. After pruning, help the bush recover and thrive by feeding it dried or composted manure (about 20 pounds for the average-sized bush). Scatter this in a circle a foot away from the bush and let a light spring rain wash it into the soil.

RENEWING AN OLD LILAC

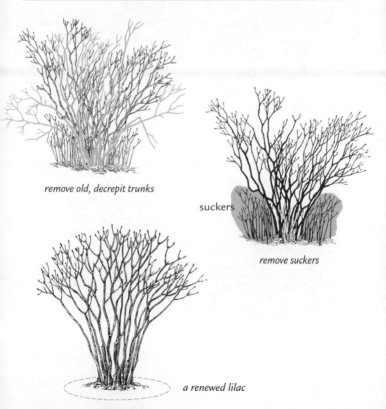

remove old, decrepit trunks

suckers

remove suckers

a renewed lilac

Q Will I hurt a flowering shrub by cutting off some blooms for a bouquet?

A No. Picking beautiful flowering stems is one of the great pleasures of growing a flowering shrub. You won't harm the plant if you cut properly, and you'll accomplish some of your pruning. Just pay attention to where and how much you cut. Here's how to thin stems for a bouquet:

◆ Whenever possible, choose blossoms growing toward the interior of the plant. This way, taking a bouquet will not be as noticeable, plus you'll be helping the plant to maintain a pleasing shape.

◆ Cut the stems to another branch without leaving a dead stub.

◆ Never tear off stems or you'll damage the plant.

◆ Although heavy picking isn't likely to disturb an older, well-established plant, cut sparingly, if at all, from young bushes.

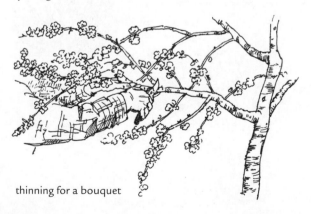

thinning for a bouquet

Q Peegee hydrangeas are my favorite shrubs, but I'm scared to prune them for fear of destroying the flowers. When can I cut them back?

A Pruning hydrangeas is unnecessary unless you want to manipulate the size and amount of flowers, control the size of the shrub, or clean out old or dead wood. The best time to prune the white- to pink-flowered *Hydrangea paniculata* cultivars such as 'Grandiflora' (peegee), 'Tardiva', 'Unique', and 'Limelight', is during dormancy, since they bloom on new wood (see summersweet question on page 98). For bigger blooms on a smaller shrub, you can prune panicle hydrangeas hard by cutting back stems to two pairs of buds early in late winter or early spring. Smooth hydrangea (*H. arborescens*) cultivars such as 'Annabelle' and pink INVINCIBELLE SPIRIT also bloom on new wood and can be pruned by cutting them back hard when they are dormant.

Q How do I prune other hydrangeas?

A Bigleaf hydrangea (*Hydrangea macrophylla*) blooms on the previous year's growth. Traditionally, you prune it after the flowers fade, from late spring to August. Doing so preserves this season's flower buds, which are mostly at the stem tips. An alternative is tip pruning in early spring to get rid of winterkill and force lateral (side) flower buds to grow for more abundant blooms.

Oakleaf hydrangea (*H. quercifolia*) needs little trimming except for taking out dead and weak stems at the base either in early spring or after flowering. Climbing hydrangea (*H. petiolaris*) flowers on old wood but rarely needs pruning. Cut back unwanted lateral shoots after flowering in early to midsummer.

Q I have the perfect spot for a hydrangea tree, but I can't afford the ones at the nursery. How can I turn a shrub hydrangea into a tree?

A Some shrubs make pleasing single- or multi-trunk trees. To start, you need just pruners and a little patience. Peegee hydrangea (*H. paniculata* 'Grandiflora', pictured here) grows quickly and eagerly and responds well to training.

Follow these simple steps to turn a multi-trunk hydrangea into a single-trunk tree:

1. The first year, prune to a single stem.
2. The second year, cut off lower branches.
3. Continue to prune off bottom branches as the tree grows taller until the desired treelike form is reached.
4. The finished product — a handsome plant, in and out of bloom.

Other shrublike trees that can be pruned to a single trunk include: Blackhaw (*Viburnum prunifolium*), buttonbush (*Cephalanthus occidentalis*), chaste tree (*Vitex agnus-castus*), Hally Jolivette cherry (*Prunus* 'Hally Jolivette'), Japanese angelica (*Aralia elata*), nannyberry viburnum (*Viburnum lentago*),

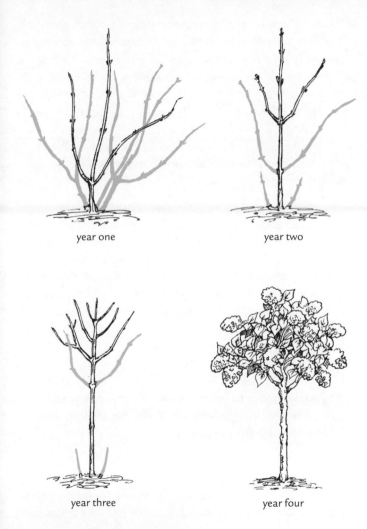

year one

year two

year three

year four

oleander (*Nerium oleander*), possumhaw, smooth witherod (*Viburnum nudum*), rose of Sharon (*Hibiscus syriacus*), sargent crab apple (*Malus sargentii*), serviceberry (*Amelanchier* spp.), Siberian pea shrub (*Caragana arborescens*), siebold viburnum (*Viburnum sieboldii*), silk-tassel (*Garrya elliptica*), wayfaring tree (*Viburnum lantana*).

Q How do I prune ornamental berry shrubs for a great display?

A Most berry-producing shrubs, such as cotoneaster, firethorn, and viburnum, need little pruning. If the fruit is important, prune lightly to keep them in shape and to correct damage caused by animals, weather, disease, or insects.

Note that some berry-producing shrubs, including bayberry and winterberry, are dioecious, meaning that plants are either male or female. For fruit production, you need both male and female plants. If you want berries, you have to plant a male among several female plants.

Q My wife likes to cut branches of holly, cotoneaster, viburnum, and other berry shrubs to decorate the house. Is this bad for the plants?

A When a plant is small, it isn't a good idea to cut off the branches, although a few berries can be snitched with no harm. As a bush gets older, however, you can gather a moderate amount of the colorful berries to use for bouquets or holiday decorations. Naturally, it is better to cut off branches with clippers rather than to break them off in jagged tears. Since most of next year's fruit buds are near the ends of the limbs, don't sacrifice too many of them.

Q When's a good time to prune ornamental fruit- and berry-producing shrubs?

A Prune them when dormant, either in early spring before growth begins or in winter after the berries have either passed their prime or been eaten by birds.

FRUIT- AND BERRY-PRODUCING SHRUBS

Prune these fruit and berry shrubs when dormant:

Bayberry (*Myrica pensylvanica*)
Beach rose (*Rosa rugosa*)
Chokeberry (*Aronia* spp.)
Cotoneaster (*Cotoneaster* spp.)
Firethorn (*Pyracantha coccinea*)
Hawthorn (*Crataegus*, best with a minimum of pruning)
Heavenly bamboo (*Nandina domestica*)
Pomegranate (*Punica granatum*)
Winterberry (*Ilex verticillata*)

Q The first few years I had my redtwig dogwood, its bright red winter color was great. Now the bark looks dark and dull. What's wrong?

A Most likely your shrub just needs pruning, because the best color appears on the new growth. To keep the stems fresh and new, some people cut back their shrubby dogwoods to 12 inches when dormant, removing that season's spring blooms. If you like the flowers, cut back the shrub every other year instead of annually. Pruning will also keep its suckering habit in check. If you prefer a more conservative approach, cut down one-third of the oldest stems every year.

SHRUBS WITH COLORFUL BARK

Careful pruning displays the bark of these shrubs to advantage; sometimes it even brightens the hues of the bark.

Bloodtwig dogwood (*Cornus sanguinea*)
Coral bark willow (*Salix alba* 'Chermesina')
Golden or yellowtwig dogwood (*Cornus sericea* 'Flaviramea' and 'Budd's Yellow')
Golden willow (*Salix alba* 'Vitellina')
Japanese clethra (*Clethra berbinervis*)
Japanese kerria (*Kerria japonica*)
Red osier dogwood (*Cornus sericea*)
Tartarian or redtwig dogwood (*Cornus alba*)
Winter jasmine (*Jasminum nudiflorum*)

Roses

Q Do all roses need pruning, including those advertised as easy to grow?

A Probably. We all want our rosebushes to live up to their full, beautiful potential. If you were to ask anyone, young or old, to name the perfect flower, it would likely be the rose. For centuries, in both legends and backyard gardens, the rose has been one of the world's most popular flowers. Contemporary breeders have developed disease-resistant roses in a wide range of shapes and colors. There are roses that bloom on bushes, vines, hedges, and even trees. Rose petals and hips are popular in teas, jellies, potpourris, and numerous other culinary and aromatic concoctions. It's only right that the rose gets special mention when it comes to pruning.

Most roses benefit from pruning. The goal of rose pruning is to promote plant health by opening the center of the plant to sun, light, and circulating air.

Q I've ordered some mail-order bare-root roses for my garden. Do they need pruning before planting?

A Depends. Roses are sold bare-root and potted. Don't prune back a potted rose; it's already established and growing. A bare-root one, on the other hand, may need a little attention, and because it is still dormant, you can cut safely. Here's what to do:

1. Once you get your bare-root rose home, soak it in a bucket of water for a few hours or overnight to hydrate it.

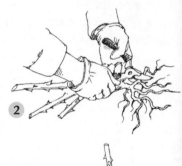

2. Check the root system, and trim off any damaged or dead growth.

3. If the plant is more than 8 inches high and has never been cut back or has been only partially cut back, cut down your rose to about 6 or 8 inches above the dark line that shows where ground level was when it was dug. Be sure to cut to a live bud or branch each time so that you leave no dead stubs.

Q Where do I make a pruning cut on a rose cane?

A Always cut on a slant just above a bud or to a live branch, and retain enough leaves and stems to feed the plant. For cutting heavy branches, you may need a saw or loppers.

GENERAL ROSE MAINTENANCE

Most roses are thorny critters, and you'll appreciate a pair of heavy gloves when you're pruning and carrying away the clippings. Be especially careful to use sharp bypass clippers so that you don't crush the stems and cause cell damage.

The kind of pruning you do, and when you do it, varies according to the classification of your rose and your climatic conditions. Hybrid tea roses need the most pruning, whereas species roses usually require very little. Although some polyantha, floribunda, and hybrid tea roses are quite vigorous, others have been weakened by hybridization and need special care, especially for the first year.

ROSE-PRUNING TIPS

◆ Hold off cutting any blooms with long stems from hybrid teas during the first year. In future years, once a plant has several strong, tall canes, moderate cutting of blooms will be fine.

◆ Cutting roses in full bloom, with long stems and some leaves, is actually summer pruning, so be sure that you don't scalp the plant.

◆ To grow a large exhibition flower, practice disbudding: pick off all the smaller buds along the stem and leave only the large, fat bud at the top.

◆ Unless you're growing a rugosa or other rose with showy hips, always snip off fading blooms, to direct the plant's energy into making buds for next year's display.

◆ Always cart away clippings from the rose garden; they can become a breeding place for diseases and insects if left on the ground.

◆ You can prune heavily those roses that grow vigorously, but cut wood sparingly from the slower-growing, weaker kinds. Heavy pruning doesn't always stimulate a weak plant to grow faster. In fact, depriving it of necessary leaf area may make it lose vigor and produce fewer blooms.

Q When should I prune my rosebushes?

A That depends upon where you live and what you want to remove. Most live-wood rose pruning occurs in early spring, just as the buds are beginning to swell. Hard frosts are usually over by this time, and the sap isn't yet flowing enough to cause a heavy loss from the cut ends. In very mild-winter climates, however, late winter is best for rose pruning. Rose gardeners traditionally prune ramblers right after they flower.

Q I'd like to try growing hybrid tea roses, but I've heard that pruning them is complicated. Should I give it a try?

A You bet! The glamorous blossoms produced on your hybrid tea will make your efforts worthwhile. Hybrid teas are the most common roses in the United States. Hundreds of named varieties are offered in catalogs, garden centers, and supermarkets every spring. You can choose from recently introduced, patented varieties or the old reliable favorites such as 'Peace' and 'Mister Lincoln'. You must prune them each year to keep them blooming well. The flowers bloom on new shoots sprouting from canes that grew the previous year.

Q What's the best way to prune hybrid teas?

A Follow these steps:

1. Thin out old, weak, and winter-damaged canes and those that cross, rub, or grow too close together. If you prefer tall-growing roses, you may not want to shorten them much except to make drooping canes a bit stiffer. If short, bushy plants fit better into your garden scene, cut the ends of the canes farther back to bud eyes where you can see some new growth. For bigger but fewer flowers, cut back stems to 6 inches high.

2. Remove suckers originating from below the graft. Take them off as close as possible to the roots or stem where they emerge. They detract from the bush's appearance and won't resemble the plant above the graft. Pruning should result in a bowl-like plant with the center open to light and air.

3. Cut back older main stems to strong new shoots.

4. Cut back to five or so strong canes, each about 10 to 18 inches above the bud union. When spring arrives, the plant will burst into vigorous new growth, and it will regain its former height come summer. If cane-boring insects are a problem for you, you can seal cuts on healthy pith with wax or white glue.

1 thin out old, weak, and
winter-damaged canes

2 remove suckers originating
below the graft union

3 cut back to strong new shoots

4 cut back to five or
so strong canes

Q My hybrid teas produce medium-sized flowers. Can I get my bushes to grow big blooms like those at the florist?

A To help your hybrid tea roses reach their full potential, pinch off side buds when they're still small, leaving only the terminal bud on a stem. (This is called disbudding.) Although you won't get nearly as many flowers as you would without pinching, each bloom will be big and gorgeous. For floribunda and grandiflora roses, remove the terminal bud, which blooms first, so the other buds in the spray will open together without having a hole in the center of the cluster. Or experiment and see what happens when you prune to a single flower.

Intervene anytime you see swelling flower buds; timing varies depending on the plant. The sooner you disbud, the faster the plant's strength will become concentrated on the remaining buds — with magnificent results.

Disbudding can also be done later, when flowers are about to go into a bouquet. Florists commonly disbud plants because sometimes one large blossom is more desirable than a lot of smaller ones in an arrangement. Professional plant exhibitors may disbud for show-quality specimens. While this technique is fun to try, especially if you like to pick flowers for bouquets, too many king-size blooms in a garden look unnatural.

disbud

Q I live in Illinois, where winters are cold. Can I grow hybrid teas, and if so, will they need special pruning?

A If you live in a cold-winter area (USDA Zone 6 and north), take steps in the fall to protect your plants. In late fall during early dormancy, prune back tall canes to about 36 inches, thus stabilizing the rose and preventing it from heaving in the wind. Cover with 12 inches of compost or topsoil, mounding over the entire base. Do this before the temperature drops below 15°F. Don't worry if all the leaves haven't fallen off. In early spring, you may still find some winter injury despite the covering. Prune any affected canes to live white pith.

Q Do I prune other roses the same way as hybrid teas?

A Each rose classification has slightly different pruning needs.

Floribundas resemble hybrid teas; however, they have several flowers in sprays rather than one to a stem, and they are generally shorter-growing. Prune them like hybrid teas. For bigger but fewer clusters, cut back stems to about 6 inches high.

Polyanthas produce clusters of small and medium-sized blooms, which are seldom disbudded. The bush needs minimal pruning; just trim to the size you choose. Remove nonflowering wood. If your polyantha shows signs of spider mites, take leaves off the bottom few inches to prevent them from getting a grip on your plant.

Q I want to plant a hedge of rosebushes. How should I prune it?

A Hedge roses need heavier pruning at planting time than do those grown as specimens in the garden. Set the plants 2 feet apart or slightly closer, and prune them to within 4 or 5 inches of the ground when you plant them. Each spring, cut back enough to produce a bushy, hedgelike effect. In summer, when bushes grow too tall or wide, snip the ends to keep the hedge looking even.

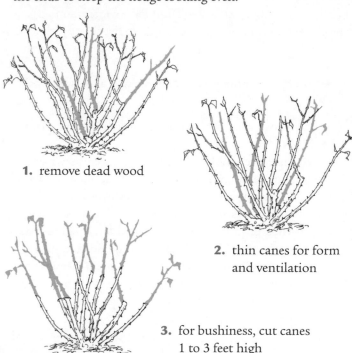

1. remove dead wood

2. thin canes for form and ventilation

3. for bushiness, cut canes 1 to 3 feet high

ROSE HIPS

Some shrub roses, especially rugosas, produce large numbers of red seedpods called hips. These are a rich source of vitamin C. Although it is better to cut off fading blooms of most roses so that bushes won't produce energy-draining hips, rugosas are so vigorous that it doesn't harm them a bit to let the hips develop. Pick off hips after a light frost, before they freeze hard and turn mushy. Among other roses with showy hips are musk rose (*R. moschata*) and sweetbriar (*R. eglanteria*).

Q How do I prune old roses, species roses, and shrub roses?

A Pruning methods for each are similar, depending upon their use in the garden and their relative vigor.

Modern shrub roses resemble old-fashioned roses and have a half-wild appearance. They can grow for years with no care at all but look their best with some attention. They are usually allowed to grow tall for a hedge effect, but if you like shorter, heavier-blooming plants, you can cut back the bush to 1 foot from the ground early each spring, before growth starts. Prune **English roses** — shrub roses combining aspects of old garden roses and modern roses — lightly or hard depending upon the vigor and desired size of the plant. The most robust varieties gain from summer pruning, cutting back flowering stems to two or three buds after each flush of bloom.

Species and old roses include moss roses, sweetbriars, cabbage roses, and rugosa roses, and they are pruned in nearly the same way. All are vigorous, so if you don't prune them annually, cutting back heavily every few years may be necessary. At a minimum, remove dead wood, some old canes, and stray long shoots every couple of years.

Q Is there a difference between climbing and rambling roses?

A **Climbers** differ from rambling roses in having a more upward habit of growth that better enables them to climb a trellis or pole. Many of the best hybrid tea roses are now available in climbing form. Their flowers are large, and they bloom for most of the summer, unlike the short blooming season of the ramblers.

Ramblers bloom once a year and are not grafted. All the new canes coming from the roots are part of the main plant, so you don't need to worry about wild suckers crowding out good canes. Let ramblers ramble. If the plant grows too thickly, cut out the oldest canes. If the plant gets too big, prune it as you would a climber. Choose ramblers carefully for size, since they are so vigorous that they can quickly outgrow their planting space and may need heavy pruning that reduces the next season's bloom.

How do I prune climbing and rambling roses?

A Just follow these simple steps:

1. For repeat-blooming climbers, remove dead and unproductive canes at the ground and cut back canes that have bloomed recently to about 6 inches. If the remaining new, strong canes still seem to be too numerous, cut out a few of these also. Aim for five strong, husky canes to remain.

2. Prune off the top few inches of any nonbranching canes. Also, snip off weak growth on the new canes.

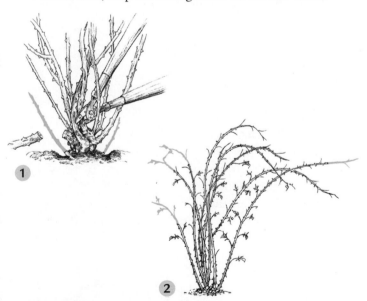

3. Prune back branches that have flowered by one-third, ending above a healthy bud or shoot.

Q What's a good way to train a climbing rose to grow on a trellis against our house?

A Climbers look better if you allow a few tall, narrow branches to reach the top of a trellis, where they can grow thickly and then cascade downward while blooming heavily. To encourage this kind of growth, remove most of the weak canes so that the plant's strength goes into the few that remain. Cut them in early spring, when the plant is dormant. Clip off fading flowers to encourage repeat blooming.

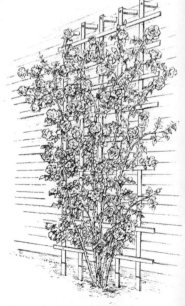

The following steps will show you how:

1. Climbing roses need good ventilation when grown against a wall. Keep the trellis at least 3 inches from the wall.

2. As they grow, tie the stems to the trellis with strips of cloth. Avoid unnecessary pruning until the rose covers the trellis.

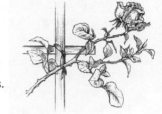

3. Steer some of the new canes to grow outward to cover the trellis early. By training some of the canes horizontally, you'll increase bud set and flowering.

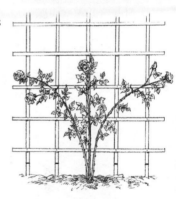

4. Continue to snip off branches that are growing too thick. Every three years, cut out a few of the older canes and allow others to replace them.

How do I keep my rose tree looking good?

 Tree roses, or rose standards, are usually hybrid tea, grandiflora, or floribunda roses that have been grafted or budded on top of a briar or rugosa rose rootstock that is 3 feet high or more. Keep rose standards healthy and attractive by removing suckers growing on the main stem or from the roots as soon as they appear, or they will crowd out the grafted rose in a short time. Follow these steps:

1. Thin out weak and/or old branches that are no longer blooming well.
2. Remove crossing branches.
3. Cut back remaining branches to 5 to 10 inches from the graft.

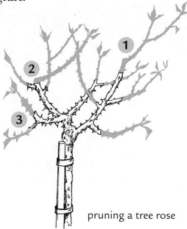

pruning a tree rose

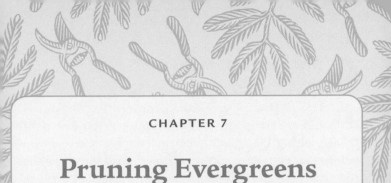

CHAPTER 7

Pruning Evergreens

Watch a hungry herd of Holsteins shear the bushy fir and spruce that dot the pastures of many northern New England dairy farms. They must be doing something right! You can see them chewing the pale green, soft new growth as soon as it appears in spring. When the short growing season is over, the cows stop snacking on evergreens and go to other fodder, enabling the cut ends to heal rapidly. Like these bovine botanists, you can trim evergreens to slow their growth. But many healthy, well-sited, well-chosen evergreens need little to no pruning to look beautiful.

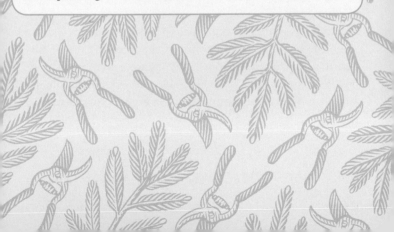

Q What exactly is an evergreen?

A Trees and shrubs are usually divided into deciduous and evergreen categories. Deciduous trees lose their foliage during the winter, whereas evergreens keep theirs year-round. Evergreens can have either broad leaves like the American holly and Southern magnolia, or narrow leaves like pine and yew. There are also a considerable number of semi-evergreen plants that are deciduous in the North and ever-green in the South.

Q If I plant evergreens around my house, where should I plant them for the best effect and the least amount of maintenance?

A Evergreens offer a home landscape many advantages. In this example (illustrated at right), large blue spruces to the northwest block cold winter winds; rhododendrons and boxwoods can grow in their shelter. On the south side of the house, evergreen trees aren't as good in the North because when they grow tall they will block the warming winter sun. But in warm climates, a Southern magnolia on the south side provides summer shade. To keep the amount of maintenance and pruning to a minimum, choose evergreens with a mature size that suits your available space.

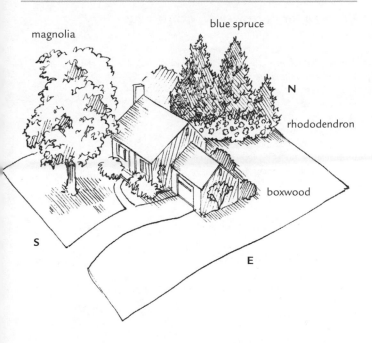

magnolia

blue spruce

N

rhododendron

boxwood

S

E

SOME COMMON EVERGREENS

Needled, or narrow-leaf, evergreens

Arborvitae (*Thuja* spp.)
California incense-cedar (*Calocedrus decurrens*)
Cedar (*Cedrus* spp.)
China fir (*Cunninghamia lanceolata*)
False cypress (*Chamaecyparis* spp.)
Fir (*Abies* spp.)
Hemlock (*Tsuga* spp.)
Japanese plum yew (*Cephalotaxus* spp.)
Japanese yew (*Podocarpus* spp.)
Japanese cedar (*Cryptomeria japonica*)
Juniper (*Juniperus* spp.)
Monterey cypress (*Cupressus macrocarpa*)
Pine (*Pinus* spp.)
Spruce (*Picea* spp.)
Yew (*Taxus* spp.)

Broadleaf evergreens

Andromeda (*Pieris* spp.)
Azalea and rhododendron (*Rhododendron* spp.), some
Bay laurel (*Laurus nobilis*)
Boxwood (*Buxus* spp.)
Camellia (*Camellia* spp.)
Cherry-laurel (*Prunus laurocerasus*)
Chinese witch hazel (*Loropetalum chinense*)
Gold-dust plant (*Aucuba japonica*)
Holly (*Ilex* spp.), some
Mahonia (*Mahonia* spp.)
Nandina (*Nandina domestica*)
Skimmia (*Skimmia japonica*)
Southern magnolia (*Magnolia grandiflora*)
Sweet olive (*Osmanthus* spp.)

Narrow-Leaf Evergreens

 How do I know when to shear evergreen hedges?

Many people think that trees grow like children — all year-round and without a pause. Needled evergreens, however, have briefer, faster growth than do deciduous trees and shrubs, which grow throughout most of the summer. For most needled evergreens, new growth occurs for only about 3 weeks, although some, such as hemlocks and junipers, have a longer season, and yews make a small additional growth in late summer where climate permits.

You need to watch for this fleeting period, because it is the ideal time to shear your evergreens. Pines, most spruces, firs, and yews begin to grow about the time that freezing nights are over and the ground is warming up (this may vary from April or even earlier in the South to mid-June in the colder sections of the country). Arborvitae, cypress, hemlock, and juniper start their growth a little later.

Fortunately, because evergreens have a built-in dormancy that is well adjusted to their locality, they seldom start to sprout much ahead of schedule each season. Even during an unusually early warm spell in winter, they are likely to wait until the proper time to start growing.

What is a conifer?

 Trees and shrubs with cones and needled or scalelike, narrow leaves are conifers. Evergreens with needles are called conifers, but not all produce typical cones. Yews and junipers, for example, produce berries. (Technically, conifers produce naked seeds protected by cones; juniper "berries" are actually modified cones.) To add to the confusion, some conifers are not evergreens. Larch or tamarack (*Larix* spp.), bald cypress (*Taxodium* spp.), and dawn redwood (*Metasequoia glyptostroboides*) have needles and bear cones but shed their needles every winter.

How often do I need to prune conifers?

Pruning makes it possible to keep a conifer at a certain size or allow it to grow so slowly that it hardly seems to be growing at all. Pruning can also turn several evergreens into a hedge or transform one into a whimsical garden accent. But once you start pruning a conifer to alter its normal growth, you have to keep pruning it one or more times a year.

If you don't have the time to prune, choose a conifer with a mature size that suits your available space and let it grow without interference. A well-sized conifer generally needs no pruning unless it has a dead, damaged, or hazardous limb. Conifers are easy to grow and, unlike some deciduous trees, don't sucker out.

ALL SHAPES AND SIZES

Choose the right-size plant for your spot to minimize pruning. The American Conifer Society classifies conifer sizes:

Miniatures grow less than 1 inch per year and are less than 1 foot tall at 10 years.

Dwarf conifers grow from 1 to 6 inches a year and are 1 to 6 feet tall at 10 years.

Intermediates grow 6 to 12 inches per year and are 6 to 15 feet at 10 years.

Large conifers grow more than 1 foot per year and are over 15 feet tall at 10 years.

Q When's a good time to prune conifers?

A You can take off a shoot or branch of a needled evergreen at any time, but the best time to prune is during dormancy or in spring as soft new shoots expand. That gives lateral (side) buds time to develop bushy growth and cover up the pruned stem's brown tip.

If your goal is controlling growth, you can wait until the growth is over but still soft in late spring or early summer, depending upon the plant. You can prune pines when the new spring growth takes the form of fast-growing, upright, light-colored shoots (candles) that are pinched to restrict the plant's size.

Shearing usually takes place in spring and early summer, when conifers are putting on the fastest growth. In the long run, shearing is harder to maintain than selective thinning, in which you remove one branch at a time. Remove dead, diseased, and damaged material at any time.

SEE ALSO: *Page 138 for candling.*

Q I just planted a spruce tree. How much should I prune it?

A Again, your goal is all-important. Unless you are training topiary, let the conifer's natural habit be your guide. If you want your spruce to keep looking like a tight, narrow cone branched to the ground, then you need to start shaping it when it's young. It is difficult to change the form of a tree once it is well established. If you allow it to grow too wide at the base, for instance, it will be very difficult to decrease the width later on without spoiling the appearance of the tree.

Q My big old juniper looks sad. Can I rejuvenate it?

A People often wonder if they can renew an evergreen tree or hedge that has grown too large and out of shape by cutting it back nearly to the ground. Although you can do this to a smooth hydrangea (*Hydrangea arborescens*) with good results, it will not work with an old and tired evergreen; you will have to replace it. Evergreens do best when you remove no more than a quarter of their bulk in any one season.

Very few conifers sprout from old bare wood. Here are a few exceptions. If you have any of the following, you can cut back even an older plant heavily and it should recover and begin to grow again:

- Bald cypress (*Taxodium* spp.)
- Plum yew (*Cephalotaxus* spp.)
- Redwood (*Sequoia* spp.)
- Sequoia (*Sequoiadendron* spp.)
- Yew (*Taxus* spp.)

 How far back can I cut a conifer branch?

That depends upon your goal and which conifer you want to prune. For the safety of people and property, for example, you may have to remove an entire branch back to the branch collar at the trunk or to another branch. For many conifers, however, cutting into bare wood behind living foliage will kill the branch. Check the Plant-by-Plant Pruning Guide, beginning on page 311, for more information.

POPULAR EVERGREENS AND WHERE TO CUT THEM

Fir (*Abies* spp.) Look carefully at the branch to locate live buds. All firs bud on new season's growth and some bud on one-year-old wood.

Cedar (*Cedrus* spp.) Like fir, cedar buds on new growth and sometimes on one-year-old wood.

Plum yew (*Cephalotaxus* spp.) Prune on old or new wood.

False cypress (*Chamaecyparis* spp.) To prune this genus, cut living foliage but do not cut back into bare wood.

Juniper (*Juniperus* spp.) Cut into branch areas producing live foliage.

Spruce (*Picea* spp.) Take stems back to a bud, which is usually on new growth but sometimes on one-year-old wood.

Pine (*Pinus* spp.) Pinch soft new growth at the stem tips, called candles, before it hardens in summer. Otherwise, prune with caution.

Douglas fir (*Pseudotsuga menziesii*) Prune or shear soft new growth.

Yew (*Taxus* spp.) Prune on old or new wood.

Arborvitae (*Thuja* spp.) Prune where there is green growth.

Hemlock (*Tsuga* spp.) Prune on old or new wood with needles.

Q Sheared conifers look unnatural to me. Is there another way I can control their size?

A Yes, there is. Most landscapes, including naturalistic ones, look better without sheared trees. For a more natural look, cut back individual branches with pruners to slow growth or produce a denser specimen.

Even if you don't need to control size, that doesn't mean you'll never have to prune. There will still be times when you need to remove woody limbs — when one dies, for instance, is diseased, or is damaged in a storm. You may also have to cut off failing lower branches shaded out by larger limbs above. Use thinning cuts as you would with a deciduous tree. For best results, remove no more than 15 to 25 percent of the total leaf area in a year, and spread out major pruning over several years. Keep the following points in mind:

1. Always cut a damaged branch back to a larger branch or a trunk.

2. Tall-growing evergreen trees look best when growing with one strong, central leader. Fortunately, this is their natural tendency. Occasionally, however, a competing leader or two will develop. To save the tree's appearance, remove the interloper, shorten it, or, if feasible, bend it down.

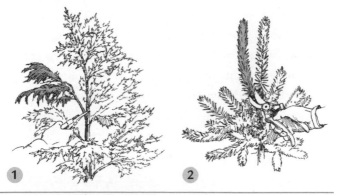

SEE ALSO: *Thinning, page 63.*

When is the best time to shape conifers?

You can actually prune conifers at any time, but some stages are easier on plants than are others.

◆ **To shorten or remove limbs,** cut them in late winter when the tree is dormant.

◆ **To shorten limbs only slightly,** do it in the very early spring so the new growth will cover your cuts within a few weeks.

◆ **To shear,** begin after growth starts in the spring.

WITCHES'-BROOMS: GOOD OR BAD?

Many dwarf and miniature evergreens derive from witches'-brooms, or genetic mutations of woody plants. A witches'-broom is a mass of congested shoots that develops from a single point in the branches of a tree. Small conifers are in such demand that horticulturists tramp through woods and pastures looking for new and interesting mutations to propagate. Witches'-brooms also occur on deciduous trees such as oaks, maples, willows, and hackberries. In hackberries, double infection by gall mites and powdery mildew fungus triggers these growths, which can be cut back if you dislike them.

Q I have a tiny yard where I grow small evergreens for year-round interest. How should I prune them?

A With the popularity of town houses and the necessity for small lots in crowded areas, demand is increasing for small landscape plants. Some evergreens, like the spreading yew, some mugho pines, and trailing junipers, grow short and shrubby naturally.

But no matter their size, some conifers still need occasional pruning. A spreading yew that is 2 feet tall and 10 feet across may look interesting on an open hillside but it will look out of place beside the front step. Remove dead and damaged material. Light pruning, such as removing stray shoots or a leader on a shrub you want to keep low, is best. Maintain spreading, creeping, or globe-shaped evergreens according to their natural growth habits. Thinning and heading back are the preferred pruning methods to use. Avoid shearing very small conifers when possible.

SEE ALSO: *Thinning, page 63 and Heading Back, page 61.*

Q I planted a pine by my driveway. It's growing so fast that I'd like to control its size. Can I shear it like a hedge?

A When pines are growing, they send out numerous little upright shoots called candles. Avoid shearing them to reduce the chance of cutting into the woody stems, where new growth will not develop. Instead, pinch, snap, or clip off one-half to two-thirds of each candle to control size. Pinching or snapping the soft new growth is known as candling.

For big jobs, use hand shears and cut into the soft new growth. Pruning with electric clippers is problematical, because shearing too deeply can kill the branch; thus a slip of the hand can ruin your plant in a flash.

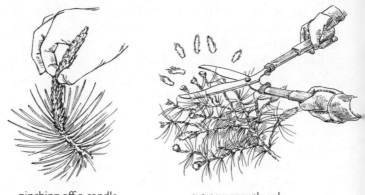

pinching off a candle   cut new growth only

Q The bottom branches on two white pines died. Can I remove them?

A Remove the dead branches. When young, many evergreens have beautiful lush branches that grow to the ground. But as the trees grow big and old, their lower branches may be shaded out and die. Trees such as Japanese red pine (*P. thunbergiana*) have such attractive bark that you may want to show it off. Think hard before cutting; once the branches are gone, you can't put them back!

If you remove lower branches on a very large evergreen, you may find that sometimes a lower limb has a large, fat, burl-like growth where it joins the trunk. If so, cut the limb just outside the burl instead of flush with the branch collar.

Q I just planted a hemlock. Should I shear it?

A Hard shearing offers maximum growth control. If you prefer not to shear severely, you can prune lightly and let your tree gradually increase in size throughout its life. For more natural landscapes, a better, more sustainable choice than shearing is to buy a conifer that matures at a suitable size for its allocated space. Then the only pruning your tree will need is the removal of the occasional wayward shoot. Read plant labels carefully, do your research, and in the long run you'll save time, money, and energy.

Q What will shearing do to my new evergreen?

A Shearing gives plants a formal look, making it a fine choice for topiary, geometrical accent plants, or refined hedges. When you shear off new growth, a tree's energy, which normally would cause the limbs to make active upward and outward growth, is redirected into the numerous side buds and twigs. The result? You control the plant's growth, forcing it to grow bushier.

Q How does shearing work?

A When you shear a plant to control its size or shape, the plant looks bushy on the outside, but behind the surface growth, just inches deep, is a larger area where vegetation has been shaded and died out. Growth is dense on the outside because shearing removes the terminal buds, thus activating dormant buds below the tips.

Terminal buds (1) are the fat brown buds that were formed the preceding year. You can spot them at the end of each twig from midsummer to the next spring. Cutting the ends of this new growth will create a denser appearance.

Dormant buds (2) are the thousands of nearly invisible smaller buds that develop on an evergreen's twigs and branches. Ordinarily they do not grow, but clipping or shearing at the proper time stops the active growth of the terminal buds and stimulates the sprouting and growth of many of the dormant buds.

Q How often do I need to shear the yews in front of my house?

A Shearing is a high-maintenance activity. Two or three shearings a year may be necessary if you want to confine your trees to a tight, geometrical form.

THREE PRINCIPLES
OF PRUDENT SHEARING

1. For best results, start small. Folks often say, "When that plant gets to the height I want, I'm going to start shearing it." This is a mistake. It is difficult, if not impossible, to get a hedge or a tall, loose-growing tree to tighten up if you start shearing too late in its life.

2. Never take off more than 15 to 25 percent of an ever-green's total green material. Bear in mind that removing more than this may damage the tree.

3. Shear every year. It is important that shearing be an annual event, because if you miss even one year's clipping, it is difficult to get some trees back into shape.

Q When should I shear evergreens?

A Begin after growth starts in the spring. Spring shearing offers several advantages:

- The small interior buds will start growing at once.
- The cuts you make on the new growth will heal quickly.
- New buds will form where the cut was made and completely hide any shearing wounds. The tree will look for all the world as if growing that way was its own idea.

Q I was too busy this spring to shear my hedge, and now it's summer. Can I shear it now?

A The answer is a qualified yes. It's fine to shear after the spring growth flush, but it's best to stop by late summer. If you wait until late in the season, the small buds you hoped to stimulate will remain dormant. You'll cut off the newly formed buds, and unsightly cut stubs may show through winter, or frost may hurt tender new growth.

Q How do I shear an evergreen tree?

A Think of shearing as giving the tree a buzz cut. Cut off the ends of all the branches on the outside of the tree, much as you would shear a sheep or a dog. Each type of evergreen grows differently: new growth on hemlocks tends to be droopy; new growth on spruce or fir is stiff. A good shearing takes only a few minutes per plant — time well spent. Look over your plantings every day or two when they are making their most active growth.

Q Which tools should I use for shearing evergreens?

A You can choose among several tools, depending upon the task you want to perform.

◆ **Long-handled hedge shears** are the best tools for shearing because they're easy to control and safe to use.

◆ **Fingers.** If you have only a few small evergreens, you can give them a light pruning by simply pinching off the ends of the soft new growth with your fingers. This pinching is especially effective on the stiff, upright candles of dwarf pines.

◆ **Electric clippers** can be a big help when you're doing a lot of shearing that must be completed early in the growing season, because they are so much faster than hand shears. They are especially good for shearing hedges.

◆ **Thin-bladed shearing knives** are good for fast work and are widely used on Christmas-tree plantations, but they are not well suited to the precision work required in home landscaping, and they can be dangerous, too.

SEE ALSO: *Shearing-Tool Safety, page 47.*

BATTLING BAMBI

In some parts of the country, deer are major pests and "prune" woody plants — even thorny ones — down to stubs. You can reduce damage by choosing species that are deer-resistant. No plants are deer-proof, though. Appetites vary from region to region, so plants that deer ignore in one spot may get munched elsewhere. Deer eat anything when hungry enough, even plants described as deer-resistant.

Q There's a blue spruce in our town square that gets sheared every spring. Why shear it when spruces look good without shearing?

A Perhaps the spruce in the town square was chosen without thought to its ultimate size. It would probably be much bigger without its annual shearing. Some evergreens grow about a foot each year. By shearing annually, you can shorten this growth to no more than a few inches per year, which appreciably lengthens the time you can enjoy the tree before it gets too big and needs replacing. Without pruning, the lower branches on spruces often die with age, and the trees form an irregular crown. Annual shearing or pruning helps counteract this tendency. Well-sheared, tight-growing trees make favorite nesting places for birds, as they like the protection of the dense branches for raising their young.

Q Which kinds of evergreen trees are best for shearing into a specimen?

A **Pines** are not ordinarily a good choice for sheared specimens because they grow fast and tend to lose their lower branches. They really look best when allowed to grow into magnificent, full-sized trees.

Firs and spruces lose their lower branches after a few years, although they make attractive temporary sheared plantings.

Arborvitae, hemlock, and **spruce** make medium-sized, stately specimens that will last a long time. They hold their branches to the ground well if you shear them regularly. If you live in the eastern United States, be aware that hemlock woolly adelgid insects endanger the health of both eastern hemlock (*Tsuga canadensis*) and Carolina hemlock (*T. caroliniana*). Mountain hemlock (*T. mertensiana*) and western hemlock (*T. heterophylla*) are not under threat.

If you determine that shearing is right for you and your plant, shear to its natural shape. Hemlock and American arborvitae grow as narrow pyramids and look best when they are sheared to this form. Spruces develop a pyramidal shape, too, but are more spreading at the base. Globe arborvitae (*Thuja occidentalis* 'Globosa') needs little or no pruning to keep its natural round shape.

prune to the natural shape of the trees

SEE ALSO: *Shaping Hedges, pages 157–164.*

Q I want to buy a Colorado blue spruce to grow as a formal, shaped specimen tree. How do I go about this?

A First, pick the right plant. Choose one with a form similar to the shape you want. At the nursery, look for a young tree that is bushy and well shaped so that you get your project off to a good start.

Here's what to do when you get home:

1. **Planting day.** Prune off any broken roots or branches.
2. **The first year or two.** Let the tree get established and prune it as little as possible, removing only dead or damaged wood.
3. **After the first few seasons.** Let your tree grow a little each year in its early life. One or two light shearings each growing season are enough, unless you are trying to achieve a highly formal look.
4. **After the tree has reached the desired size.** Depending upon the kind of tree, severe shearing once a year can probably keep it from getting larger, though more than one light shearing may be necessary during the growing period.

Q Can I dwarf a full-size conifer by pruning it?

A Yes, but . . . if you want to grow dwarf evergreens, it is better to buy and plant true dwarfs than to continually shear tall-growing specimens. Not only do real dwarf plants look more natural, but they're also easier to care for, and there's less danger that they'll outgrow the spot you've given them.

If you want to keep a spruce, fir, pine, hemlock, or arborvitae to a height of 1 or 2 feet for a lifetime, follow the instructions for shearing specimen trees. Instead of one or two light shearings each year, however, you will need to give the tree a tight clipping every four or five days during the growing season. Shearing must be especially severe once the tree reaches the desired height to keep it small. Root pruning every few years is another way to slow down the top growth and make shearing easier and more effective.

Q What can I do about my creeping juniper, which outgrew its space?

A When a plant exceeds its allotted space — like this juniper, which has wandered into the sidewalk area — you will have to prune it back. Just prune it at the time that will cause the least trauma to the plant: late winter to early spring.

Cut to live wood when possible. There may be times, however, when you must prune to a spot without foliage for safety's sake. That wood will not regrow, so make sure that enough live wood grows above the cut to creep over it.

Q I have an arborvitae screen on my property line, and I like the privacy it gives us. How do I keep it dense?

A Spruces, arborvitae, and hemlocks make ideal screens or windbreaks because they grow slowly and tight and hold their lower branches to the ground longer than do faster-growing pines and firs.

147

Once your arborvitae screen has been in the ground for a year or two, you can clip the top and sides annually for a few years. This helps the plants grow in tight and close to the ground. Keep the sides sheared so the width will be manageable. Make sure that the top part of each tree is narrower than the bottom, because lower branches need all the light they can get.

Broadleaf Evergreens

Q Do broadleaf evergreens need much pruning?

A Broadleaf evergreens generally need little pruning, and the pruning they do need is similar for all of them.

Azalea (*Rhododendron* spp.), holly (*Ilex* spp.), mountain laurel (*Kalmia latifolia*), and rhododendron grow throughout much of the United States, while bay laurel (*Laurus nobilis*), holly, mahonia, some jasmine (*Jasminum* spp.), oleander (*Nerium oleander*), sweet olive (*Osmanthus* spp.), gold dust plant (*Aucuba japonica*), and olive (*Olea europaea*) grow in the warm South and along the Pacific Coast. In addition to these, many shrubs are deciduous in the North and evergreen in the South, such as certain varieties of abelia, andromeda (*Pieris* spp.), azalea, barberry (*Berberis* spp.), cotoneaster, daphne, euonymus, pyracantha, privet (*Ligustrum* spp.), and some viburnums. Most of these are sold potted or with their roots in a ball of soil, so no pruning at planting time is necessary.

Q When's the best time to prune my broadleaf evergreens?

A As with many other woody plants, you can snip an overlong stem or remove dead, damaged, or diseased material at any time. Do major corrective pruning of broadleaf evergreens from late winter to early spring, before new growth starts.

For the best floral display year after year, prune springflowering broadleaf evergreens after blooming, before the plant has set the next year's flower buds.

Q How do I prune my rhododendron?

A Snip off the terminal, or end, buds of the new sprouts to force the buds to develop and grow along the sides of the branches. After the plant reaches blooming size, if the branches are growing too long, you may pinch off the small end buds. Be careful to leave the big fat blossom buds that will be next spring's blooms. If you want your bush to stay compact, continue pruning back to a lateral (side) bud or branch inside the crown for the life of the plant. You will be the proud owner of a handsome, bushy, vigorous shrub.

Prune most broadleaf flowering evergreens the same way, except for plants that grow leggy, like heavenly bamboo (*Nandina* spp.). Cut back a few of the oldest, tallest stems each year to promote new leafy shoot growth.

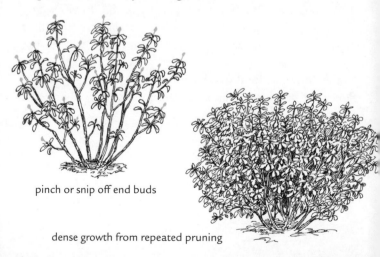

pinch or snip off end buds

dense growth from repeated pruning

Q I just planted two azaleas and a rhododendron. Do I need to train them?

A Azaleas, mountain laurels, and rhododendrons are closely related, so their pruning the first few years after planting is much the same. Often they have a loose habit of growth. Early pruning to train young plants is important if you want a tight, compact bush. Pinch or cut back an inch or so of new growth at the stem tips above a set of leaves in early summer.

Q When should I prune camellias?

A Camellias also need some pinching of the end buds in early summer if you want to the plants to grow bushy. If you prefer a particular shape, perhaps tall and narrow against the house, cut out the shoots that are growing in the wrong direction. Train the longer shoots by carefully bending them and tying them to a lattice or a trellis in the way you want them to grow.

SEE ALSO: *Espalier, starting on page 179, and page 22 for disbudding camellias.*

Do I have to prune my hollies?

Holly needs very little pinching when it is young, since it tends to grow tight naturally. Some folks shear Japanese holly to a particular shape. If you are growing a holly hedge, it will need an annual clipping during the growing period. If you prefer your holly to grow tall, however, prune it as little as possible until it reaches the height you want. This may take a few years, so be patient. Stems of red-berried hollies such as American holly (*Ilex opaca*) make attractive holiday decorations. Remember that every time you cut branches for decoration, you are actually pruning, so be mindful of where and how much you cut.

I planted a holly by the front porch. Now it's huge. Do I have to get rid of it or can I cut it way back?

As broadleaf evergreen shrubs grow older, they can outgrow their space, get tall and leggy, or just need rejuvenation. In the South, rhododendrons, azaleas, mountain laurels, and hollies are often pruned back anywhere from 1 to 4 feet from the ground to renew them.

Spreading out heavy cutback over three years, especially if below-freezing temperatures are common where you live, is usually better for the plant. Remove one-third of the biggest, oldest stems each year until you've renewed the whole plant. Do heavy pruning of this type in late winter or very early spring.

Q Should I deadhead my rhododendrons?

A Remove fading flower trusses of rhododendrons immediately after they have bloomed so that the plants won't waste their energy setting seeds. This process is called deadheading.

Q What are some pruning tips for maintaining broadleaf evergreens?

A Remember, broadleaf evergreens need little pruning. Just keep track of their size relative to their space and watch for dead, diseased, or damaged wood.

- Shorten (head back) any branches that are too long in spring.
- Cut off winter injury and broken branches anytime.
- Go easy on picking flowers for bouquets from small plants during the first few years. Once they're mature, you can safely cut flowers from mature plants in moderate amounts with no damage to the plants.

Woody Herbs

Q I grow herbs among perennials and flowering shrubs in my garden beds. Do they need annual pruning?

A Most of the woody herbs, such as lavender (*Lavandula* spp.) and rosemary (*Rosmarinus officinalis*), need little pruning other than shaping and removing old or injured parts. The tall-growing ones, such as bay laurel (*Laurus nobilis*), benefit from an occasional cutting back to control size, especially when they are grown as houseplants.

You can also shear woody herbs into formal hedges or topiary forms. Pruning techniques such as pinching back, disbudding, and deadheading can improve the looks and life of your woody herbs.

Q When should I prune shrubby herbs?

A A good time to prune is early spring, just as new growth begins. Save the trimmings for drying or for starting new plants. Before buying shrubby herbs for your garden, make sure they can survive in your area. Even where the plants are hardy, severe winters may cause dieback of stems or whole plants.

CHAPTER 8

Pruning Hedges

The way you prune a hedge varies according to its purpose. You can trim it into a tight and formal shape or allow it to grow loose and natural. You can make it tall, medium, or short — or, if you want, you can sculpt the top into towers and turrets. If you're starting from scratch, you can create an evergreen or deciduous hedge, or one that produces fruit or flowers.

Caring for a hedge is not difficult, yet as you drive around, it's obvious that many gardeners are not skilled in the art. Just like an old-time barber may want to trim a stranger's long wild hair, keen gardeners feel the urge to stop their cars, grab their shears, and start clipping an overgrown, neglected hedge.

Q What are some ways I can use hedges in my garden?

A Hedges of various kinds are important landscape additions. You can use a hedge to (**1**) create an attractive border or backdrop, (**2**) mark property lines, (**3**) shield out traffic noise and fumes, (**4**) hide unattractive views, (**5**) discourage trespassing (human and animal), (**6**) ensure privacy, (**7**) form windbreaks or snow traps, and (**8**) shelter nesting birds.

Q I just planted a hedge. Do I need to prune right away?

A To encourage bushiness to the ground, cut back any tall shoots or broken roots on container-grown shrubs (don't prune side shoots) at planting. For the first year, limit other pruning to removing broken branches. The larger the initial leaf space, the faster the tree will settle in.

If you're planting some bare-root decidu- ous shrubs, cut them back by one-third after planting to promote bushiness and low branching.

Shaping Hedges

Q When should I start pruning a new hedge?

A You can begin shearing in the second or third year. Even if you want your hedge to grow to 4 feet, don't wait until it gets to that height before you start to shape it. In order to have a tall, tight hedge, you should first develop a *small,* tight hedge and then let it grow larger gradually. Just as it is difficult to make a single, tall, loose-growing tree compact and bushy, it's no easy job to tighten up a large, loose-growing hedge.

Q What's the correct way to shear a formal hedge?

A The amount of shearing depends upon the specific plant and whether the hedge is formal or informal. You'll need to trim an informal hedge only once or twice a year, although more vigorous growers, such as privet and ninebark, may need additional clippings. Formal hedges need even more attention during their growing season, especially fast growers; clip while new growth is less than 12 inches and remove stray shoots as needed. Shearing hedges is easy if you follow these guidelines:

◆ Always shear a hedge so that the bottom is wider than the top. Otherwise, lower branches, lacking their full share of sunlight, will thin out and soon die. The difference may be barely noticeable, but it is extremely important.

◆ Unless you have an excellent eye for such things, you should use a template or put up posts and a string as a guide when you're shearing long, straight, formal hedges, so that you don't end up with a lopsided row.

◆ Don't shear off the top of a hedge and ignore the sides. Soon it becomes irregular and too wide and sags under the weight of heavy rains, ice, or snow. If anything happens to an individual plant, you can replace it much more easily if your hedge is slender.

Q Last winter, heavy snow ruined my beautiful flat-topped hedge. Is there another shape that would work better?

A Hedges with rounded or pointed tops work best in snowy winter sites. Snow can squash a flat-topped hedge under its weight. Follow these tips for good-looking hedges:

A box effect (**A**) works best where snow loads are not too heavy. Keep the bottom slightly wider than the top, so all branches get sunlight.

If sides are too straight (**B**), the lower branches may not get enough sunlight and thus die out.

In areas with heavy snows, round off the top of the hedge to help it shed snow, as in shapes (**C**), (**D**), and (**E**).

If you want a more informal look, avoid shearing; instead, clip individual branches as needed to control size (**F**).

The top of hedge (**G**) is too wide, making this shape undesirable — the sun can't reach lower limbs and snow will crush the top.

hedge shapes

TIMELY TIPS FOR SHEARING

◆ Most needled evergreens make their growth early, so
you won't need to shear them after midsummer.

◆ Prune most deciduous plants, like privet, ninebark,
and barberry, after the spring growth flush. They
grow for a longer period, so you can trim them off
and on for much of the summer, depending upon the
formality of the hedge.

◆ Broadleaf evergreens such as boxwood and Japanese
holly also grow over a long period, so hedges may
need some clipping throughout the season.

◆ Prune flowering hedges directly after the blooms have
faded so that new buds can set for the following year.
(Rose hedges are the exception and are best pruned
in early spring or late fall. Prune back in the summer
only if they are growing too tall or too wide.)

Q I have both holly and forsythia hedges bordering my
yard. When is the best time to prune them?

A Prune forsythia and most flowering hedges right after
bloom, before plants form buds for next year's flowers.
The best time for trimming hollies and most nonflowering
hedges is after the plants make their fastest growth. This varies with the type of plant. Do not prune in late summer and
fall. New growth may not harden, making plants vulnerable to

winter damage. This holds true for both formal and informal hedges. If you have plenty of space, forsythia makes a glorious big hedge when planted at a distance from the house and left to keep its natural arching form.

Trim your hedge when it looks like it needs it. Just as you wouldn't wait for your lawn to become a field before mowing it, you shouldn't plan to trim your hedge just once during the growing season. Not only will repeated trimming make it thicker and better looking, but it will also be healthier because it will expend less of its energy on useless growth. If your hedge needs more than a trim, wait until plants are dormant (late winter to early spring, before growth starts).

Q I'm planting a hedge between the front and back yards. How can I go from front to back without leaving a gap in the hedge?

A A big gap can look awkward. For a more graceful effect, why not make an arch in your hedge? Whether you choose a hedge archway or one made of vines, you should shear or clip it every year so it grows thick and bushy. If you keep the sides narrow enough to allow light to enter, the branches on the underside of the arch will stay green and growing. You can also train a freestanding arch over a flagstone path as a garden accent.

- ◆ **The simple method:** Plant two tall-growing trees 4 to 6 feet apart to act as the sides. (*Note:* They should be far enough apart so that by the time they have grown thick and full, you will still have enough room to walk or take a lawn mower through the opening.) In the spring, when they are starting to grow actively, bend them over carefully to the desired height and tie them together to form the arch. Within a few years, they will grow together.

◆ **Cheating:** Build a wooden trellis in the proper shape and plant a vine to cover it. If you choose a compatible vine, it will look very much like a part of the hedge.

A homegrown arch

Q We stopped pruning an old hedge a few years ago. How do we revive it so we can put the house on the market?

A You may be faced with an overgrown hedge, with plants that are too tall, too wide, or growing out of kilter with each other. If the plants are healthy, you can sometimes cut them back nearly to the ground and allow them to start over. Your chances for success are best with a deciduous hedge — privet, ninebark, pyracantha, potentilla, lilac, bayberry, or spirea, for example.

You can also cut back and renew certain evergreens. Yew, boxwood, and holly will often respond well to a severe pruning. But spruce, pine, fir, and hemlock can seldom be rejuvenated in this manner, and arborvitae will survive a hard pruning job only if the plants are young. If your overgrown hedge is made of these evergreens, either shape into a tall, informal hedge or take them out altogether and start over with new plants.

Q Which cutting tools can I use to clip a hedge?

A Electric hedge shears make hedge trimming simple. They're fast, easy to handle, precise, and less tiring to use than hand shears. However, hand shears with long handles and blades are excellent if you don't have to shear a great deal. A shearing knife is convenient for informal shearing but not accurate enough to use for formal work.

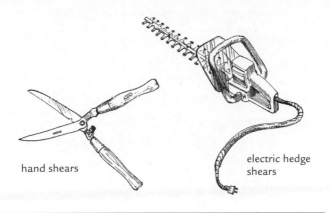

hand shears

electric hedge
shears

Types of Hedges

Q I'd like to use formal hedges to divide my garden into separate outdoor rooms. Which plants are best?

A Although the formal, European style of landscaping is rarely used around American homes these days, tightly clipped hedges are still popular. Some favorites are:

- Arborvitae (*Thuja* spp.)
- Boxwood (*Buxus* spp.)
- European hornbeam (*Carpinus betulus*)
- European beech (*Fagus sylvatica*)
- Holly (*Ilex* spp.)
- Japanese pittosporum (*Pittosporum tobira*)
- Japanese yew (*Podocarpus* spp.)
- Yew (*Taxus* spp.)

INVASION OF THE ALIENS

Some popular landscape plants, including several privet species and Japanese barberry, are now considered invasive in many parts of North America. Invasive plants are introduced species that spread aggressively; they endanger native plant species and threaten wildlife habitat. Check with your local Cooperative Extension Service to see if the following plants are troublesome in your area; if they are, choose alternatives for your garden.

Japanese barberry (*Berberis thunbergii*) is invasive in at least 20 states, including all of New England and the Mid-Atlantic. Many states ban the sale of common or European barberry (*B. vulgaris*), another invasive, since it is an alternate host for wheat rust and a serious threat to agriculture. Common barberry is present in most of North America.

If you want to grow barberry, use noninvasive species. A good one is William Penn barberry (*Berberis × gladwynensis* 'William Penn'), a spiny, 4-foot rounded shrub hardy in Zones 5–7 (and some parts of 8) with glossy evergreen foliage that turns reddish bronze in fall. A taller alternative (8 feet high and wide), wintergreen barberry (*Berberis julianae*), has clusters of yellow flowers in spring and black oval fruit frosted white in fall; it is hardy in

Zones 6–8 and some parts of Zone 5. Either species
makes a tough informal barrier hedge. Substitute purple-
leafed wiegela for Japanese barberry's purple cultivars.

Many species of privet (*Ligustrum*) are invasive. Chinese
privet (*L. sinense*) is a weed throughout the southeastern
United States, and European privet (*L. vulgare*) has
seeded itself into the eastern United States and several
states farther west. Some good substitutes are American
holly (*Ilex opaca*) and blackhaw viburnum (*Viburnum
prunifolium*).

Some vines are also invasive. Among them are Orien-
tal bittersweet (*Celastrus orbiculatus*), English ivy (*Hedera
helix*), Japanese honeysuckle (*Lonicera japonica*),
and silver lace vine (*Fallopia baldschuanica,*
formerly *Polygonum aubertii*).

barberry (*Berberis vulgaris*)

privet (*Ligustrum vulgare*)

Q Our house sits on a busy corner and we want people to stop cutting across our lawn. What would make a good barrier hedge around our property?

A Sometimes folks plant hedges to keep out unwanted visitors, human or animal. Living fences are often cheaper to establish and maintain than real fences, and they appear less hostile.

In time and with careful pruning, most plants can be grown into a barrier hedge, but dense, thorny, rugged plants are best if you have a choice. Clip or shear your plants in the summer, when they are actively growing. Do it once over lightly — just enough to produce a thick, informal hedge — or frequently and severely to achieve a neater, more symmetrical, and more formal appearance. In either case, follow the general rules for shearing, and never allow a plant to grow wider at the top than at the bottom. These barrier hedges are favorites:

- Beach rose (*Rosa rugosa*)
- Colorado blue spruce (*Picea pungens*)
- Firethorn (*Pyracantha coccinea*)
- Flowering quince (*Chaenomeles* spp.)
- Hawthorn (*Crataegus* spp.)
- Holly osmanthus (*Osmanthus heterophyllus*)
- Osage orange (*Maclura pomifera*)
- Variegated five-leaf aralia (*Eleutherococcus sieboldianus* 'Variegatus')
- William Penn barberry (*Berberis* × *gladwynensis* 'William Penn')
- Wintergreen barberry (*Berberis julianae*)

SEE ALSO: *Shaping Hedges, starting on page 157.*

Q I need a hedge but I don't want a green wall. What are my options?

A Ordinarily, plants don't produce flowers or fruit well when they're sheared into a tight hedge pattern. But many flowering shrubs work well as a hedge if you allow them to grow naturally, pruning to encourage denser growth and to remove weak or crossing branches rather than shearing. The following make beautiful informal, lightly pruned hedges:

- ◆ Buddleia (*Buddleia spp.*)
- ◆ Cotoneaster (*Cotoneaster* spp.)
- ◆ Crab apple (*Malus* spp.)
- ◆ Firethorn (*Pyracantha coccinea*)
- ◆ Forsythia (*Forsythia × intermedia*)
- ◆ Glossy abelia (*Abelia × grandiflora*)
- ◆ Honeysuckle (*Lonicera* spp.)
- ◆ Lilac (*Syringa* spp.)

- Mock orange (*Philadelphus coronarius*)
- Oleander (*Nerium oleander*)
- Rose (*Rosa* spp.)
- Saint-John's-wort (*Hypericum* spp.)
- Viburnum (*Viburnum* spp.)

Q My job and family chores don't leave me much time for gardening. What are some low-maintenance plants I can use for hedging?

A Gardeners with limited time, or those who don't especially like to putter around the garden, may prefer to have hedges that require little care. Informal hedges need less maintenance than formal hedges. Consider a mix of flowering shrubs rather than just one type of plant.

If you don't mind a little pruning, choose plants you can clip quickly and easily. Upright-growing shrubs with fine twigs and small needles or leaves are easier to trim than coarser-limbed, spreading varieties or those with larger leaves or longer needles.

A young, growing hedge needs less attention than a mature hedge that has reached the size you want. Often one annual pruning is enough for evergreens in their formative years, but after the hedge is mature, one heavy pruning and a few additional light ones over the course of a season may be necessary to keep it looking good.

LOW-MAINTENANCE HEDGES

A Few Good Evergreen Choices

Arborvitae (*Thuja* spp.)

Cherry laurel (*Prunus laurocerasus*)

Glossy abelia (*Abelia* × *grandiflora*)

Holly (*Ilex* spp.)

Inkberry (*Ilex glabra* 'Compacta')

Littleleaf boxwood (*Buxus microphylla*)

Spruce (*Picea* spp.)

Upright yew (*Taxus cuspidata* 'Capitata')

A Few Good Deciduous Choices

Crab apple (*Malus* spp.)

Forsythia (*Forsythia* × *intermedia*)

Hedge cotoneaster (*Cotoneaster lucidus*)

Hedge maple (*Acer campestre*)

Koreanspice viburnum (*Viburnum carlesii*)

Renaissance spirea (*Spiraea* × *vanhouttei* 'Renaissance')

Rose of Sharon (*Hibiscus syriacus*)

Summersweet (*Clethra alnifolia*)

Q How can I keep my informal flowering hedge attractive as it matures?

A When flowering shrubs become too straggly, remove some stems to the ground or cut back the branches to an outward-facing branch or bud at different heights inside the crown. The shrubs will grow fuller and more compact. This care is especially important to keep plants looking nice in hedges and borders.

CHAPTER 9

Artistic Pruning

Artistic pruning makes an animal from a shrub or a cloud from a tree. It can also turn a fruit tree that would grow 25 feet wide into a freestanding narrow fence or a candelabra grown against a wall. With pruning, you can even change a tree into a shrub with much larger leaves or form living walls on tree trunks above the ground.

Although fancy topiary and other art forms demand patience and skill, the simple shearing of evergreens and the shaping of flowering shrubs and fruit trees are so easy that anyone can have fun with the process. Many varieties of dwarf plants are ideal for artistic shaping because they grow slowly. Nor do you have to sacrifice practicality. Some commercial orchardists grow trees as sheared hedges, cordons, and fences — forms that are traditionally considered more ornamental than useful.

The pruning of an artistic form must continue during the life of the plant. Snipping and shearing will be part of your summer chores, just like mowing the lawn and pulling weeds in the garden. If you spend years creating a horticultural masterpiece and then neglect it and go on to other projects, you'll find that within a year or so it's overgrown and probably past help. But such is the life of a gardener — a thing of beauty is a job forever.

Topiary

Q What's it called when a bush is turned into a sculpture?

A The art of trimming trees and shrubs into geometric forms, arches, animals, and many other shapes is called topiary. Shearing reaches its zenith in this form of artistic pruning. European topiary started around the time of Julius Caesar. Since then its popularity has waxed and waned, but it remains a formal garden feature on both sides of the Atlantic. Some Americans keep spiral topiaries in pots near the stoop, and you can now buy these ready-made. Creating topiary can be lots of fun. Potential shapes are limited only by your patience and imagination, and sometimes by your climate.

Q Does pruning fancy topiary take a lot of time and effort?

A Artistic pruning requires your time throughout the growing season. Most of the shearing must be done in early summer, when the trees and shrubs are growing fast, so if you like to scuba dive in Aruba or fish in Alaska in May or June, this hobby isn't for you. You'll need to be in your garden several days a week when the plants are growing, if only for a few minutes each time.

I'd like to try my hand at making a whimsical topiary. Where on earth do I begin?

 Start with small, tight-growing plants. Plant them in an area where they will receive a full day of sunlight.

Begin shaping after the first year or so, when the plant is still small. You can't take a large tree and sculpt it into an artistic shape like an artist chiseling away at a block of marble.

Shear as soon as growth starts and continue as long as necessary throughout the summer. The amount of shearing depends upon the plant you choose to train. Some evergreens need two or three shearings a year; deciduous plants have the advantage of growing faster and producing quicker results but they need more shearing. You want to create a closely grown, tiny-leafed (or needle) effect.

Shear your basic shape (for example, a cone or pyramid), allowing bulges to appear gradually. Shape a bulge into a head, or leg, or other part of your design.

How do I make a simple geometric topiary?

Follow this three-step method:

1. To create a three-tier geometric topiary, start with a tree that will grow to a shape similar to the form you want to create. Shear it all around.

2. Begin to remove unwanted branches between sections.
3. Clip remaining branches into globes or cubes, the largest ones on the bottom.

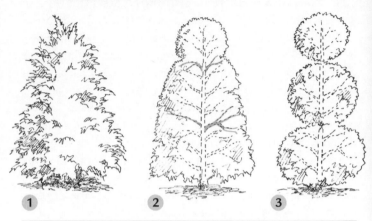

1   2   3

Q At Disney World I loved the character-shaped shrubs in big pots. How would I make something like that?

A More complicated forms — four trees that form the legs and body of Jumbo the elephant, for instance — require careful planning and usually a framework of wood or metal. Some gardeners train English ivy (*Hedera helix*) over topiary frames instead of training shrubs to grow through the frames. To make your own:

1. Buy a preformed frame or make your own.
2. Plunge a stake or pole into the ground as close as possible to the middle of the young plant and secure the frame to the stake at some point. Otherwise, the frame

may shift over time and make it difficult for you to keep to your original plan.

3. Wait for stems to emerge beyond the frame's bounds, then clip them back neatly, or, if you want them to expand laterally to fill in the shape, tie them loosely to the frame with soft twine.

Q I live in Minnesota. Is making topiary possible in my cold climate?

A Most topiary is grown in warmer zones, where snow can't crush it. If you live in the North and want to experiment, remember:

- Use only the hardiest plants. Native species are usually best.
- Select topiary shapes that are pointed or rounded on top and narrow in width, so they won't collect heavy loads of snow and ice.
- When winter comes, build a wooden tepee around fragile pieces, or plan on removing the snow as soon as possible after each big storm.

Q Which plants make the best topiary?

A Evergreens are the usual choice for topiaries large and small. However, you can train the crowns of some deciduous trees into less intricate shapes such as globes, cubes, cylinders, arches, and free forms.

GOOD CHOICES FOR TOPIARY

Evergreen

Boxwood (*Buxus* spp.)
Dwarf Alberta spruce (*Picea glauca* 'Conica')
Holly (*Ilex* spp.)
Ivy (*Hedera* spp.)
Japanese podocarpus (*Podocarpus chinensis*)
Juniper (*Juniperus* spp.)
Loropetalum (*Loropetalum chinense*)
Olive (*Olea europaea*)
Rosemary (*Rosmarinus officinalis*)
Sweet bay (*Laurus nobilis*)
Yew (*Taxus* spp.)

Deciduous

Apple and crab apple (*Malus* spp.)
European beech (*Fagus sylvatica*)
Hedge cotoneaster (*Cotoneaster lucidus*)
Hedge maple (*Acer campestre*)
Hornbeam (*Carpinus betulus*)
Japanese zelkova (*Zelkova serrata*)
Little-leaf linden (*Tilia cordata*)
Thornless honey locust (*Gleditsia triacanthos* var. *inermis*)

Q How do I turn a rosemary into a lollipop tree?

A Follow the directions on pages 104–105 for turning a shrub into a tree. Once your rosemary has reached the height you desire, clip or shear the top growth into a globe shape. You'll need to clip or shear several times a year to maintain the size and shape.

This lollipop form of shrub or small tree is known as a standard. Tree roses are another form of standard. Other common choices for standards are lavender, bay laurel, and dwarf citrus.

Espalier

Q If I had room, I'd grow an orchard in my tiny city garden. Is there some way I can squeeze in one fruit tree?

A You don't need an orchard to grow your own fruit. With an espalier, even people with tiny yards can grow apples, pears, peaches, and other kinds of fruit almost flat against a wall, fence, building, or trellis. An espalier is a tree or shrub trained to grow in a two-dimensional pattern rather than in the round. *Espalier* may also refer to the support on which the pruned plant grows. And it's not only fruit trees that grow on an espalier. Firethorn's brilliant berries and evergreen camellias with their elegant blooms look stunning when espaliered.

A decorative espalier shaped like a fan or candelabra makes an effective focal point in a small garden.

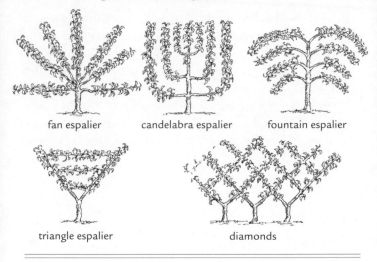

fan espalier   candelabra espalier   fountain espalier

triangle espalier   diamonds

Q What kind of support do I need for an espalier?

A Install a trellis or wire fence at least 6 inches away from a wall or fence. Galvanized 14-gauge wire is easiest and usually most practical for fruit trees. Shrubs are best trained on a trellis or lattice. Set two sturdy posts, 7 or 8 feet tall, at the expected outside spread of the espalier. Brace them to prevent the wires from sagging. Next, staple smooth wire from one post to the other like a wire fence, or screw eyebolts into the posts and thread wire through each bolt, wrapping the ends around the taut wire five or six times. Attach wires about

18 inches apart, starting 18 inches from the ground and continuing to the desired height of the espalier. Use a level to keep the tiers horizontal.

Q I love crab apples but have no room for a full-size tree in my little courtyard. Can I grow one as an espalier?

A Certainly. This special technique is not as difficult as you may think, but it does require diligence. For best results, install the support before you plant (see the previous question) and start training while the crab apple is still quite young. Here's how:

1. Select a dormant whip (a rooted, unbranched shoot) of your chosen tree. Or, some nurseries sell small espaliers that they have started to train. Although a head start may help you, there are benefits to making your own. You get your choice of plants, choose your own design, and save money.

2. Plant the tree or shrub next to a stake, keeping the bud union a couple of inches above the ground if the tree is grafted. Lightly attach the whip to the stake with twine in a figure-8 loop, which you can loosen as the trunk increases in size. Once the design is established, you can remove the stake.

3. Clip off the top of the dormant shoot just below the bottom wire. The cut should be above two buds on either side of the stem.

 Q Are successful espaliers all about pruning?

A No. Climate also matters, because it affects plant choice and growing conditions. In fact, the right setting may enable you to grow an espalier where a freestanding tree can't survive. The following tips explain how to tailor an espalier to your environment.

IN A WARM CLIMATE

◆ Grow your espalier in a spot that does not receive direct sun all day; a wall reflects heat, which will cause the leaves and fruit to suffer on hot days.

◆ A white wall is preferable as a growing background because it reflects heat away from the plant.

IN A COOL CLIMATE

◆ The more sun, the better.

◆ A dark-colored wall, such as red brick, attracts heat and is a nice backdrop.

◆ A fruit tree or vine may grow as an espalier against a wall when it would struggle growing in the open. For example, you can often cultivate grapes in a cool climate if you train them against a dark, south-facing building, whereas it would be impossible to ripen them a few feet from the building.

Q How do I turn a three-dimensional tree into a two-dimensional diamond pattern?

A Here's how to train a diamond-shaped espalier. The crossing pattern comes from the crossing branches of trees planted side by side.

1. When growth begins on your new plant, train one shoot upright and two to either side. Rub, pinch, or clip off all other shoots throughout the growing season.

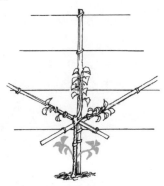

2. Bend the branches as they grow — while they are still pliable — and secure them with twine looped loosely in figure-eights to the supporting wire or trellis in your chosen pattern. Pinch back long shoots on the limbs.

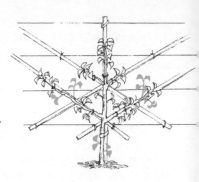

3. Above the first tier of branches, remove shoots on the trunk until it reaches the second tier. Repeat step 1 to continue the design on the second level and each year afterward until the espalier is complete. When your tree reaches the top tier, cut off the top of the trunk, retaining a branch on either side to end the pattern. It may take years to finish a complicated design. Carefully remove stakes, using soft loops (not wire) to attach the trunk and branches to the tiered support. Each year, check the loops and prune off stray shoots and dead, diseased, and broken branches.

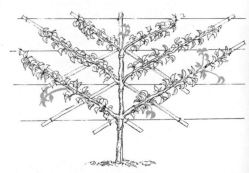

Q I want to grow an apple tree as an espalier. What do I need to know?

A Fruit-tree espaliers need special treatment. Follow the rules for pruning your particular fruit tree but keep these additional tips in mind:

- Along with the regular pruning of a fruit tree, you may need to prune off some of the fruit buds in late winter to prevent overbearing. If too may fruits set anyway, thin them out in early summer, when they are still small, so the tree will produce a crop annually.

- When you're trimming, don't cut off the short, stubby spurs that bear the fruit! Flowering crab apples and hawthorns need to have their older spurs thinned out occasionally, as they get too numerous, but always leave enough to produce a good crop.

Q Which plants make good espaliers?

A Fruit trees make good espaliers because they are both productive and pretty in leaf and in flower. Espaliers of apple and crab apple (*Malus* spp.), pears (*Pyrus* spp.), citrus, and fig (*Ficus carica*) are common and easy to train. Plums, cherries, peaches, and apricots (*Prunus* spp.) are more difficult to train, as are bush fruits and nut trees. Sheltered fruit espaliers ripen earlier than those grown in the open, which are subjected to cooling winds.

Japanese maple (*Acer palmatum*), camellia, blue Atlas cedar (*Cedrus atlantica* 'Glauca'), cotoneaster, flowering quince (*Chaenomeles* spp.), forsythia, ginkgo, hawthorn (*Crataegus* spp.), holly (*Ilex* spp.), winter jasmine (*Jasminum nudiflorum*), bay laurel (*Laurus nobilis*), magnolia, firethorn, yew (*Taxus* spp.), and viburnum are among ornamentals you can use this way.

Avoid plants that grow vigorously, such as common lilac (*Syringa vulgaris*) and hydrangea. Keeping them pruned to a strict form would be a chore.

Cordon

Q I saw a group of beanpole fruit trees at a nearby orchard. What are they?

A They are cordons, among the most popular espaliers. *Cordon* is the French word for "cord" or "rope" and refers to a planting (usually a dwarf fruit tree) that extends in a ropelike fashion, either vertically or horizontally. Europeans have used this method of creating beanpolelike fruit trees for centuries. Now Americans practice the technique.

Some commercial orchardists grow fruit trees as upright cordons because they take up so little space and come into production faster. Fruit growers, for instance, plant as many as 60 dwarf cordons to the acre; compare that with 35 full-size trees. The initial cost of buying, planting, and training is high, but subsequent pruning, insect and disease control, and harvesting costs are lower. Moreover, the planting starts producing good crops many years sooner than a regular orchard.

To make owning a vertical cordon even easier, nurseries sell Canadian and European apple tree varieties selected for their ropelike habit.

Q What do I need to know to grow a cordon?

A Several factors contribute to a cordon's success:

- Choose an upright-growing tree or shrub that will not grow too tall or too fast. Dwarf apples and pears are good candidates; the stone fruits (peaches, plums, and cherries) and citrus fruits are more difficult to train as cordons.
- For easy reach, limit the growth of the main trunk to a height of about 6 feet.
- Cordons must be kept to a manageable size, but as the roots grow, this becomes more difficult. If necessary, slow down the growth by pruning the roots (by cutting around the tree; see Root Pruning, pages 68–76).
- In addition to regular pruning of a fruit tree, you may need to remove some of the fruit buds in late winter to prevent overbearing. If too many fruits set anyway, thin them out in early summer,

cordons take up little space

when they are still small, so that the tree will produce a crop annually.

◆ Growing a cordon horizontally or obliquely — angles contrary to the plant's normal growth habit — requires heavy pruning to keep the plant attractive.

Q How do I create a cordon?

A Follow these steps:

1. Start with a branchless tree seedling. Some nurseries sell young trees with no side shoots. Plant as usual, and then prune back the top by about a third, cutting to a good fat bud. If you are working on a little tree with some side shoots, cut them off close to the trunk, leaving a single, straight whip.

2. Place a sturdy stake close to the newly planted tree but without damaging its roots. Tie the tree to the stake with soft cloth or twine at regular intervals.

3. Clip or pinch all the new growth coming from the sides to 4 or 5 inches in length. Always snip off any growth beyond the 4- or 5-inch limit on the side branches.

Coppicing and Pollarding

Q My neighbor has a golden catalpa shrub about 7 feet tall with big yellow leaves. I thought catalpas were trees. What's going on?

A This is called coppicing, also known as stooling. Coppicing is a technique whereby you regularly cut a tree or shrub to ground level, resulting in a flush of new stems from the base.

You can do the same thing in your garden. Plant a seed or seedling of golden catalpa (*Catalpa bignonioides* 'Aurea'). Let it grow for a year or two to get the roots established, then cut it to the ground after the first hard frost, when the foliage browns. In spring, new shoots will appear. You can let them all grow and turn your tree into a giant shrub or you can select a few straight shoots and eliminate the rest so that it resembles a multistem tree. Or play around and try something different every year. When you cut this tree to the ground each fall, you sacrifice the flower clusters and cigarlike seedpods, but you gain a tropical-looking conversation piece with gigantic leaves!

Q What are some reasons for coppicing?

A Gardeners coppice for many reasons. In past centuries, it was done to produce copious branches for firewood.

Now it's usually done for aesthetics:

- ◆ to renew an old shrub (such as a hydrangea)
- ◆ to turn a single-trunk tree into a shrub
- ◆ to stimulate new colorful growth on shrubs such as redtwig dogwood (*Cornus alba*) and red-stem willow (*Salix alba* 'Chermesina')
- ◆ to promote big, tropical-looking leaves on trees such as empress tree and Indian bean tree (*Catalpa* spp.)
- ◆ to encourage shoots of large, handsome juvenile leaves on purple smoke bush (*Cotinus coggygria* 'Royal Purple')

COPPICING TO RENOVATE A HYDRANGEA

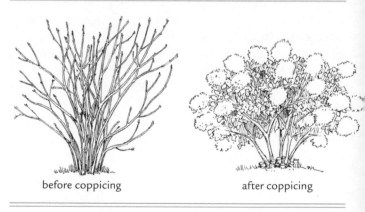

before coppicing   after coppicing

 When should I coppice a plant?

 To reduce shock to the plant, cut only when the tree or shrub is dormant.

Q What are some plants I can coppice?

A Several trees besides the catalpa mentioned on page 189 stand this treatment well. Try it on hornbeam (*Carpinus betulus*), redbud (*Cercis* spp.), and linden (*Tilia* spp.).

Some shrubs with colorful bark require periodic coppicing to maintain their color. Examples are the various species of red-twigged and yellow-twigged dogwoods and coral bark willow (*Salix alba* 'Chermesina'). Coppicing can also be done on smokebush (*Cotinus coggygria*) and yew (*Taxus* spp.)

You can coppice for practical reasons. Basketmakers use it to get flexible willow stems. Traditionally it was done in Europe to produce firewood. Poplar, willow, wild cherry, wild plum, and black locust can withstand this treatment. When harvested in the dormant season, these trees will regrow a new crop of wood in a decade or so.

Q Deer overrun my property. Is there a pruning technique that can keep them from eating my trees and shrubs?

A Try pollarding, a shaping technique that results in a formal, mannered look, like coppicing above the ground. Pollarded trees typically have thick trunks and high rounded crowns when in leaf. In dormancy, the crowns look knobby and misshapen — a beautiful-ugly aesthetic when done right. Originally used for renewable crops of firewood and fodder, this technique offers gardeners a way to regulate the height and crown size of certain vigorous trees, whether they're part of a street planting or single specimens near a porch or patio.

Proper pollarding may extend the life of a tree and keeps new growth beyond the reach of deer and other grazers. To pollard a tree or shrub, begin when the plant is young and small. First, decide upon a size and form for the tree, then sculpt it through early and consistent pruning. To maintain the form, prune new shoots to the established framework each year.

a mature pollarded tree

 What are some good plants for pollarding?

Some trees used for pollarding are fast growers like linden (*Tilia* spp.), catalpa, horse chestnut (*Aesculus hippocastanum*), and London plane tree (*Platanus* × *acerifolia*).

Q How do I pollard a tree?

A This technique may seem complicated in the beginning, but once you catch on, it's easy to maintain. Here's how:

new pollard

1. When dormant, remove the low limbs on the trunk of a small young tree to create a high crown. Head back the leader and lateral limbs to stubs to shape a framework for the pollarded tree. The framework can have one or more stems.

2. Shoots will sprout from dormant buds below these cuts in the spring. If shoots occur on the trunk or branches beyond the cut, remove them immediately. The next year, in late winter or early spring, cut off that year's growth as close to the original cuts as you can.

3. Over time, woody fists will develop at the cuts. Each year during dormancy, remove shoots close to these knobs but avoid cutting into them and thus harming the tree.

remove last year's shoots from fists

CHAPTER 10

Pruning Woody Vines and Ground Covers

Vines and ground covers are useful additions to home landscaping. Some plants can be used for both purposes: vining ivies, woodbine, and honeysuckle, for instance, also make useful ground covers. You can keep most of them looking good and under control with minimal care. The care and pruning of each is similar.

Vines do not grow quickly to just the right height and then stop growing and look nice forever after. Nor does a ground cover exist that will spread over a lawn within a few weeks, stay neat, and stop growing at the edge of flower beds, without ranging into the vegetable garden or the neighbor's putting green.

Some vines, such as wisteria and climbing hydrangea, are hardy, woody plants. A few vines have roots that are hardy and tops that are not. Tender vines, such as star jasmine, often grow this way in the North but are entirely perennial in the South. Some, such as grape, develop large trunks when very old; others, like ivy, have thin, wiry stems and can trail over brick walls. Some small, woody bushes such as creeping junipers and prostrate rosemary make good ground covers.

Woody Vines

Q What are some different ways that I can use vines in my landscape?

A **Vines as blinds.** Some people grow vines to disguise a rainspout, telephone pole, or other unsightly object. Twining vines such as variegated kiwi, star jasmine, and wisteria are ideal for this purpose because they are vigorous growers. Just remember to keep the vine well groomed and to prune it to keep it within bounds. Otherwise, the cover itself can become unattractive, defeating the purpose of improving the site's appearance.

Vines as hedges. In areas where a hedge would take up too much valuable space, vines make a good substitute. Install a woven-wire fence with well-spaced and well-braced posts and plant tight-growing vines along its length. In a few years, you'll have an effective barrier. Shear occasionally to keep the plants confined to the fence.

Q Do vines with edible fruits need special pruning?

A You must prune more precisely when your vines are growing food, and give them proper growing conditions. Most food plants, including grapes (*Vitis* spp.), dewberries (*Rubus* spp.), and kiwis (*Actinidia* spp.), need plenty of sun, so never allow the vines to become thick and overgrown. Because grapes and berries produce best only on year-old wood, you should cut away all wood older than that every year if food is your primary interest.

SEE ALSO: *Pruning Bush Fruits, Brambles, and Grapes, pages 267–294.*

Q It seems as if most woody plants need some early training. Is that also true of woody vines?

A Some early pinching and snipping adds considerably to the general appearance of most vines. Form a mental image of how you want yours to look in its prime, then prune it that way. For example, wisteria is an attractive flowering vine, but it can also be pruned into an equally beautiful shrub or small tree.

Q When's the best time to prune vines?

A When in doubt, prune woody vines when they are dormant. Clip off stray shoots and dead or diseased wood in any season.

Q I just planted a passionflower vine. Do I need to prune it?

A Potted vines need little to no pruning when you plant them, unless you need to trim a broken stem. If you're planting a bare-root, woody vine — that is, one with a hard, woody stem — you should cut the top back by about 25 percent, to a bud, on planting day. This early pruning will promote branching while slowing top growth until new roots can supply enough energy to support the growth, resulting in a more vigorous vine. Of course, carefully follow all the other proper planting procedures regarding location, planting depth, watering, fertilizer, and soil.

Q My sweet autumn clematis grows like crazy and needs cutting back. When's the best time to prune it?

A The time varies according to what you're doing. Follow these tips:

- **Do radical pruning only when vines are dormant.** That's true even for vines with the rankest growth that can withstand the hardest cutback.

- **Trim during the growing season.** After the vine has reached the height and width you want, most of your pruning will consist of snipping back any growth that goes beyond those limits. Specifically, shape spring bloomers right after flowering and late-season bloomers when dormant, in late winter or early spring.

- **Promptly remove dead and damaged wood.** Occasionally thin out some old wood to keep the vine from choking itself. Also, prune out any part of the vine that has been hurt by winter damage, been eaten by insects, or shows signs of disease. Don't neglect this chore, or eventually you will be faced with a major, tedious job.

Q How do I rejuvenate an overgrown vine?

A Radical pruning is justified when a vine has gotten completely out of control, grown way beyond its bounds; no longer looks healthy and attractive — and the prospect of going in and removing all the deadwood is overwhelming.

1. Cut back the whole plant but leave a few young stalks (year-old spurs are best), if there are any, growing near the main stem. Most vines are extremely resilient and will bounce right back.

overgrown vine in need of drastic pruning

cut-back vine

2. When the vine begins to send up new shoots, clip off most of them, leaving only three or four of the most vigorous. These will grow rapidly, and soon you will have a full-sized, healthy new vine.

199

Q When should I renew an overgrown wintercreeper?

A The best time is very early in the spring, while the vine is still dormant, so regrowth can start soon after.

Q We want to paint our house, which has a trellised magnolia vine growing up on one side. Can we cut the vine to the ground to get it out of the way?

A No. If you want to save the plant, plan your project for early spring or late fall, when the pruning will be least harmful. If you must do the job in midsummer, keep the cutting to the barest minimum to prevent a lot of late-summer regrowth.

1. Unless the vine is very stiff and brittle, cut off just enough to loosen it from its support and lay it down carefully on the ground.

loosen vine from support

2. Protect the vine while you work, and don't pile any materials on it. Put a corral of boards or bricks around it, or lay a tarp loosely over it — anything that prevents you from trampling it.

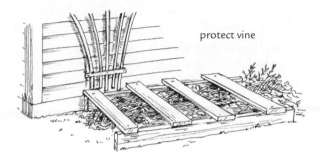

protect vine

3. Return the vine to its upright position as soon as the job is finished and tie it to its support until it anchors itself.

restored vine

Q Do I need to know how vines grow in order to prune them?

A Yes. The need for pruning often depends upon the way a vine grows and especially how it climbs. Some clinging vines, for instance, grow so heavy that their tendrils can't support them. For more details about specific vines, see the lists at right and the Plant-by-Plant Pruning Guide, page 311.

- ◆ **Ramblers.** Some so-called vines, like climbing and rambling roses (see page 121), produce long canes that should be tied to or interlaced with a trellis for support.

- ◆ **Twiners.** Many vines, such as honeysuckle and morning glory, twine around a post or wire and wind their way upward.

- ◆ **Clingers.** A few vines cling, holding on in several different ways. Some attach themselves by springlike tendrils; grapes and clematis grow in this fashion. Vines with tendrils need something to wrap around and are not too adept at climbing stone and brick walls. Virginia creeper and Boston ivy are better at that. They hang on with small sucker disks that attach firmly to a hard surface. Climbing hydrangea, wintercreeper, and English ivy can also cling to smooth surfaces, but instead of the sucker disks, they grip with many small rootlets.

A VARIETY OF VINES

Ramblers

Fourth of July rose (*Rosa* 'Wekroalt'), climber
Lady Banks rose (*R.* 'Lady Banks'), thornless rambler
Memorial rose (*R. wichuraiana*), rambler
Prairie rose (*R. setigera*), climber

Twiners

American bittersweet (*Celastrus scandens*)
Five-leaf akebia (*Akebia quinata*)
Kadsura (*Kadsura japonica*)
Kiwi (*Actinidia* spp.)
Magnolia vine (*Schisandra propinqua*)
Silver lace vine (*Fallopia baldschuanica*)
Star jasmine (*Trachelospermum jasminoides*)
Trumpet honeysuckle (*Lonicera sempervirens*)
Wisteria (*Wisteria* spp.)

Clingers

Boston ivy (*Parthenocissus tricuspidata*)
Clematis (*Clematis* spp.)
Climbing hydrangea (*Hydrangea petiolaris*)
Cross vine (*Bignonia capreolata*)
Grape (*Vitis* spp.)
Ivy (*Hedera* spp.)
Passionflower (*Passiflora caerulea*)
Trumpet creeper (*Campsis radicans*)
Virginia creeper (*Parthnocissus quinquefolia*)
Wintercreeper (*Euonymus fortunei*)

Q If I plant ivy to green up the walls of my house, will it need much pruning?

A Yes, so don't do it! Vines that cling to smooth surfaces grow well with little training, support, or other care on brick and stone structures in climates where they are perennial. They are *not* a good choice for wooden buildings like yours because they hold moisture, thus rotting the wood and making painting projects difficult. If you really want a woody vine near the entry, a trellis planted with clematis and a climbing hybrid tea rose would be better than English ivy or Boston ivy. For easy maintenance, hinge the trellis at the base and set it 4 to 6 inches from the wall to protect your home.

Q What do I need to know to grow twining vines such as kiwi, star jasmine, and silver lace vine?

A The twining vines can wind their way up wires, trellises, and water spouts. They are not good choices for planting to cover walls or brick buildings, but they make ideal screens on porches and fences. Some vines twine from left to right; that is, counterclockwise as you look down at them — bittersweet and Chinese wisteria, for example. Others, such as honeysuckle and Japanese wisteria, twine from right to left (clockwise).

Q My husband and I would like to grow wisteria on our house. How often should we prune it?

A Asian wisterias are extremely vigorous, too vigorous to grow on a trellis attached to your house. Instead, try Kentucky wisteria (*Wisteria macrostachya*), a lovely, showy but less robust vine. The cultivar 'Clara Mack' produces bloom clusters up to 14 inches long. If you like Japanese wisteria, grow it on a sturdy pergola by one of your doors, where the flowers can dangle in spring, and prune it annually.

Q Would growing wisteria on wires attached to the house make it easier to prune?

A Yes. For wisteria and other heavy vines, wires are stronger, and you can install brackets to hold them. No matter what you plan to train the vine on, always space it about 6 inches away from the wall to allow for good air circulation. Set out vines at least a foot from the support to give them room to expand.

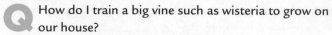

Q How do I train a big vine such as wisteria to grow on our house?

A Once you have a sturdy support, follow these steps:

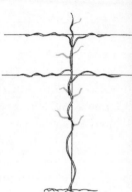

1. **Establish a framework.** While the vine is growing to the desired height, take time to train side branches (to reduce crowding, allow about 1½ feet between them). Tie them at intervals to the wires. Once the main leader reaches the height you want, chop off the top or train it to one side.

2. **Prune back side shoots.** Keep your plant in bounds and encourage bushy growth by cutting back horizontal-growing stems by about half. Do this in early to midsummer, while the wisteria is actively

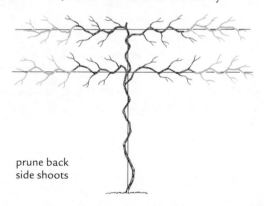

prune back
side shoots

growing. Main branches can also be shortened by about half, but it's better to do this more substantial pruning in late winter.

3. **Prune to encourage flowering.** Once you train the vine to the height and shape you want, confine all major pruning to winter or early spring, before growth starts. Cut back all shoots to four or five buds and remove suckers that appear at the base, particularly on grafted plants. Don't fertilize, as this leads to lush foliage at the expense of flowers. (If your wisteria still doesn't bloom after years of this regimen, consider root pruning — see page 68.)

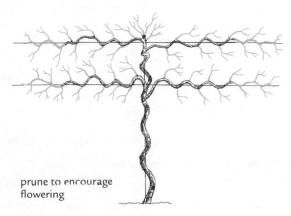

prune to encourage
flowering

Clematis

Q My clematis isn't blooming. What am I doing wrong?

A You probably pruned at the wrong time. You need to know the blossoming habit of your clematis (see the next answer). Also make sure to plant clematis where it will receive sufficient sunlight and to provide proper care in the form of regular watering, fertilizing, and liming if needed. If the plant is still shy, judicious pruning may help your plant grow better and begin to bloom.

If you're starting from scratch, here's how to encourage the most blooms. In the first year after planting, keep your clematis cut back to about 2 feet high to balance growth and encourage stem development at the base and branching. The next year your clematis may reward you by growing thick and blooming all the way up a trellis or post. If base shoots fail to develop the first year, you may need to keep the plant pruned short for a second growing season.

Q When do I prune my clematis?

A It depends upon which clematis you grow. Clematis fall into three pruning groups:

Group A (or 1) blooms in early spring on old wood (last year's stems) and needs little pruning to keep it in shape. To keep the plant small, prune out flowering shoots right after blooming. Don't cut into very old wood because it may not resprout. This group includes species such as *Clematis alpina* and *C. montana*.

Group B (or 2) blooms on old and new wood, with a flush of large flowers in late spring or early summer and a lesser display later on. In early spring, remove dead, weak, or damaged shoots to a pair of vigorous buds. Train stems that are left to the support. Old-fashioned 'Nelly Moser' is in Group B, along with 'The President', 'Duchess of Edinburgh', 'Belle of Woking', and 'Mrs. Cholmondeley'.

Group C (or 3) blooms later, in summer or fall, on new growth. To keep

know your group before you prune clematis

these shapely, in early spring prune the plant hard to about 12 to 18 inches high, taking off last year's growth. A popular example is sweet autumn clematis (*C. terniflora*) — 'Comtesse de Bouchard', 'Gipsy Queen', 'Ville de Lyon', and 'Mme. Edouard Andre' — and Jackman clematis (*C. jackmanii*).

Q I don't like where my clematis is growing. Can I move it without hurting it?

A If you ever have to move a fragile clematis vine, pruning will make the job easier and more likely to be successful. In early spring, cut the vines to within a foot or two of the ground. Dig all around the plant roots, and move the entire root-ball — soil and all — disturbing the roots as little as possible. On an older plant, the root-ball may be nearly the size of a bushel basket. If you manage to save most of the roots, and if the vine has been cut back, survival is practically assured.

Q Are special considerations needed when pruning clematis in a cold climate?

A In cold climates, clematis need protection. Prune to get the vine off the trellis, lay them on the ground, and cover them for winter. Work carefully to salvage as much of the vine as possible. In the spring, reattach and prune away winter injury.

Choose a variety that blooms on the current season's growth, because even if it is covered, a hard winter may kill the vine to the ground. Avoid pruning in late summer or fall.

Q My trumpet creeper has gotten so big that I'm afraid it's going to pull over the pergola where it grows. What can I do?

A Pruning won't harm your vine, so give that a try before you resort to digging it out. Trumpet creeper is a clinging vine. Some clingers (bignonia, clematis, passiflora, grape) grow with small tendrils that grasp wire, trellises, or other plants. Others (trumpet creeper, English ivy, climbing hydrangea, Boston ivy) have small sucker disks or rootlets, known as holdfasts, which clamp onto brick, stone, or concrete. Some clinging vines have vigorous tendrils and can support a great weight; others require occasional pruning or the weight of the vine will become too much for the tendrils to bear. Snip away large masses of dangling green, in any case, for a better appearance.

Woody Ground Covers

Q Do I have to prune cotoneaster?

A Woody ground covers such as cotoneaster usually need very little care, which is one of the main reasons we plant them — to avoid mowing steep or unsightly places. Occasionally, though, it's necessary to remove competing weed and brush growth or to cut out dead or damaged parts. Shear or clip plants that grow along paths, terraces, steps, and borders as needed to keep them within bounds.

Q My ivy is taking over. How do I control it?

A Some woody ground covers such as ivy, Virginia creeper, and bittersweet are rank growers that need frequent attention unless they have lots of room to spread. Pinch back modest plantings or use shears, an edger, or your lawn mower as needed. Install metal or plastic edging, bricks, or stone to save time. Chop back large masses when they get badly overgrown; the plant will renew itself in short order. If you have trouble keeping aggressive ground covers or vines under control, consider replacing them with less vigorous spreaders.

A FEW GOOD WOODY GROUND COVERS

Bearberry (*Arctostaphylos uva-ursi*)
Climbing hydrangea (*Hydrangea petiolaris*)
Coral honeysuckle (*Lonicera sempervirens*)
Cotoneaster (*Cotoneaster* spp.)
Heath (*Erica carnea*)
Heather (*Calluna vulgaris*)
Ivy (*Hedera* spp.); avoid *H. hibernica* and *H. helix* cultivars
Juniper (*Juniperus* spp.)
Lowbush blueberry (*Vaccinium angustifolium*)
Memorial rose (*Rosa wichuraiana*)
Trumpet vine (*Campsis radicans*)
Virginia creeper, woodbine (*Parthenocissus quinquefolia*)

CHAPTER 11

Pruning Fruit Trees

Pruning fruit trees differs from pruning shade trees. Although all trees benefit from a strong framework of branches, fruit trees in particular need well-attached branches that can carry heavy loads of fruit without breaking under the weight. Fruit trees also need air and sunlight to penetrate the branches for best health and fruit set. High humidity can lead to diseases, which you can prevent by removing branches to admit moving air and light into the crown.

Your fruit tree almost always consists of two parts. The roots usually belong to a type of tree that produces low-quality fruit but grows vigorously and is winter-hardy, whereas the grafted top is a named variety like 'Delicious'. The two are joined because this is the most efficient way to produce large numbers of quality fruit trees. Fruit trees grown from seed seldom resemble the parent tree even slightly, and growing trees from cuttings or layers is a slow and difficult process.

Q Why do fruit trees need pruning?

A Proper pruning can strengthen the structure of a fruit tree, increase its crops, and extend its life. Here are seven more reasons to prune:

- ◆ To train into a good fruit-bearing form
- ◆ To expose branches to light
- ◆ To encourage good crops of quality fruit
- ◆ To support the weight of those fruits on the limbs
- ◆ To manage a tree's size
- ◆ To keep a tree healthy
- ◆ To repair a tree that hasn't been pruned properly or at all

neglected fruit tree
in need of pruning

Q What are the basics I need to know to prune fruit trees?

A Follow these general principles. Also see specific recommendations for different types later in this chapter.

- **Keep in mind an image of the mature tree** as you clip or snip off the buds or tiny twigs. Aim to develop a strong tree with a branch structure sturdy enough to hold up the crop.
- **Prune in accordance with the tree's natural growth habit.**
- **Thin!** Keep the branches sparse enough for fruit to get enough sunlight to ripen. Some trees grow twiggy naturally; certain apple varieties, such as 'Jonathan', and many varieties of cherries, plums, peaches, and apricots need additional thinning of their bearing wood to let in sunshine.

Q Won't cutting off branches hurt my fruit tree?

A Correct pruning will benefit your fruit tree. To produce good fruit, a tree needs plenty of sunshine, and a fruit tree has a potentially large area to produce fruit: a full-sized, standard apple tree can be well over 30 feet wide and 35 feet high. However, because of its tight branch structure, only 30 percent of an unpruned tree gets enough light and another 40 percent gets only a fair amount of light. As these statistics indicate, when only the top exterior of the tree produces good fruit, you're getting the use of but one-third of your tree, and all that fruit is grown where it's most difficult to pick! Even the most careful pruning won't bring the light efficiency to a full 100 percent, but you can greatly increase it.

 Can I grow fruit trees as ornamentals in my garden?

Fruit trees are not usually recommended strictly as ornamentals. Many other flowering trees need less care and have fewer disease and insect problems.

If you want to enhance your yard with a small flowering tree and also want to grow your own fruit, visit an orchard to see whether you like the look of trees pruned for fruit production. Many people like the look of fruit-bearing trees; a commercial orchard in full bloom is a wonderful sight. And fruit-bearing species are a frequent subject for artistic pruning techniques such as espalier.

Many people think a fruit tree doesn't need much special attention when grown for looks rather than food. This isn't totally true: all fruit trees need occasional pruning to remain healthy, even if you never eat their produce. If at any time your tree, regardless of its size or age, appears to be setting too many fruits, thin each cluster of small fruits to a single fruit.

SEE ALSO: *Espalier, page 179.*

Timing

Q When is the best time to prune cherry trees?

A The simple answer: If you prune your trees regularly each year, late winter is a good time to prune. But this is a subject of ongoing debate among pomologists — those involved in the science of fruit cultivation. Seasonal conditions vary greatly throughout the country, so your location is an important factor in determining when you should prune. Also, what happens when you prune at different seasons affects the decision of when to prune. For stone fruits such as cherry, apricot, almond, peach, and plum, the best time to prune is very late winter to early spring, or from March to bloom. Pruning earlier makes them vulnerable to infection from a canker disease.

Q Should I prune my pluots and other fruit trees in spring?

A Most people agree that pruning a fruit tree right after it leafs out in spring is one of the worst times. Infections such as fire blight are most active and likely to spread in the spring. The tree will probably bleed heavily, which many people consider unsightly.

If a source suggests pruning in early spring, the author often means late winter — that is, before any sign of growth appears. The only pruning you should do after trees leaf out is to remove branches broken by storms or injured by the cold.

Q Which pruning tasks can I do in early summer?

A Avoid major pruning in early summer. Remove suckers, water sprouts, and branches too low on the stem as soon as you notice them.

Fruit trees grown in planters or tubs, espaliers, and other artistically shaped trees need more attention than do other fruit trees. They should be pruned regularly to keep them looking their best. Clip or pinch back new growth on tight hedges, cordons, and fences as soon as they begin to grow, and continue throughout the summer to maintain them in the intended size and shape.

Q Is midsummer pruning good for my pear tree?

A By pruning when new growth is several inches long, you will limit tree growth (unlike dormant pruning, which increases vegetative growth such as water sprouts). Restrict summer pruning to cutting or rubbing off suckers, unless you are following an alternative style of pruning (see the box on the facing page). Finish summer pruning by July 31 to reduce the possibility of winter injury, though exact dates vary by location.

LORETTE PRUNING

An alternative method for pruning fruit trees replaces the usual late-winter or early-spring work with pruning during the active growth season. For that reason it is sometimes called summer pruning. The Lorette method, developed in Europe by Louis Lorette, is an excellent but complicated system for intensive fruit growing. It is especially useful on dwarf fruit trees and on trees grown as espaliers, cordons, hedges, and fences.

To prevent useless limb growth, begin pruning in early summer and continue until early fall. No dormant pruning is done at all. By frequent clipping and pinching, you direct a tree's energy into producing fruit buds near the trunk or on a few short limbs, rather than out at the ends of long branches.

This technique is somewhat like shearing a hedge, and results in small, easy-to-care-for trees that bear fruit at an early age. Each part of the tree is in full sunlight because leaf area is limited. Therefore, the fruit is of superior quality.

In cold regions, the Lorette method is risky; trees pruned in summer tend to keep growing later in the season, and this growth may be injured during the winter. For the same reason, even in places where the growing season is long, vigorous-growing trees such as peach and apricot are often difficult to grow by the Lorette system.

Q Is it okay to prune my apricot tree in late summer?

A Yes, depending upon where you live. The best time to prune these trees is July or August, because that's when disease-causing bacteria are least likely to enter the pruning wounds. In warm areas, prune these trees in July and August. In cold locations, July pruning is better because it gives new growth time to harden off before frost and reduces the chance of winterkill.

In general, some people prefer to prune fruit trees in late summer. By pruning after the tree has completed its yearly growth and hardened its wood, yet before it has lost its leaves, you'll stimulate less regrowth and fewer water sprouts. You still have to remove dead or diseased branches in late winter, but late-summer pruning works well if extensive winter damage is not likely.

Q Can I prune apple trees in late winter along with my shade trees?

A Wherever growing seasons are short and you expect extreme cold or heavy snow and ice loads to injure your trees, late winter pruning is best. The trees are dormant, and since the leaves are off, it is easy to see where to make the cuts. You can also avoid cutting deeply frozen wood and causing winter damage.

However, if you have neglected your trees for a few years and they are badly in need of a cut-back, avoid doing it all at once. Excessive pruning in late winter stimulates a great deal of upright growth the following spring and summer because a tree tries to replace its lost wood. Branches, suckers, and water sprouts are likely to grow in abundance. If major pruning is necessary, you're better off spreading out the pruning over a few years. Cut off suckers and water sprouts by midsummer to eliminate that vegetative growth.

Pruning Styles

Q I'd like to try my hand at growing some fruit trees such as peach, apple, and pear in the backyard. Do I prune them all the same way?

A Different pruning styles evolved from the different growth habits and crops of various fruit trees. The canopy of a well-developed cherry or peach tree is naturally vase shaped, whereas pears are pyramidal and apples are pyramidal, rounded, or spreading, depending upon the variety. (Citrus is a special case; see page 222.) The pruning styles build on these shapes, improving branch strength and light penetration for better fruit set. The three main pruning styles are central leader, modified central leader, and open center. Here's which one to use for which tree:

CENTRAL LEADER. A pyramidal shape; best for dwarf and semi dwarf trees, not standard-sized trees

- ◆ Apples
- ◆ Cherries
- ◆ Pears
- ◆ Persimmons
- ◆ Plums

MODIFIED CENTRAL LEADER. Best for standard trees; easier alternative to central leader style for dwarf and semidwarf trees

- Apples
- Apricots
- Cherries

- Pears
- Persimmons
- Plums

OPEN CENTER (also known as vase or open-top).

- Almonds
- Apricots
- Cherries
- Crab apples
- Figs

- Nectarines
- Peaches
- Plums
- Quince trees

Q Should I prune my new citrus tree into the same shape that I prune my apple tree?

A No. Citrus trees have strong wood and they bear heavy loads of large fruits without breaking under the weight. They need little or no pruning to let in light; they make fruit in all but the darkest part of the interior. Nor does pruning affect fruit quality. Remove water sprouts and suckers from both young and mature trees, along with dead, diseased, rubbing, and broken wood. You may have to remove the occasional weak branch from little trees. Sometimes the interior of a tangerine tree gets so dark that it stops bearing fruit; it needs a little thinning. That task can be tricky because of the potential for sunscald (bark) and sunburned fruit.

SEE ALSO: *Pages 243–244 for sunscald.*

Q I want to buy some fruit trees. Should I buy standard trees or dwarf varieties?

A Standard-sized fruit trees can grow 30 to 40 feet or more. A tree that large is difficult to manage and dangerous to work in. Moreover, because so much of it is shaded, it often produces poor fruit. In suburban and urban settings, trees may be deprived of light as buildings, high fences, and other trees crowd them. They respond by growing too tall — and require a lot of drastic pruning later on.

Many fruit trees sold today are dwarf or semidwarf, rather than full-sized trees. Although the tops of these small trees are the same variety and produce the same size fruit as ordinary trees, their special rootstock keeps them from getting large. Dwarf and semidwarf trees vary from about 5 to 12 feet high when fully grown, depending on the kind of rootstock. Dwarf and semidwarf varieties not only save space (most fruits require two trees for pollination) but also reduce the amount of time and effort needed for pruning.

Q I just bought a peach tree at my local nursery. Does it need special pruning at planting time?

A If your new tree comes enclosed in a ball of soil or growing in a pot, no cutback should be necessary except to remove dead or damaged branches and any encircling roots.

HOW TO SHAPE FRUIT TREES

Central leader

WHY: With one strong trunk in the center of the tree, well-spaced branches can grow at fairly wide angles and safely bear abundant loads of large fruit.

HOW: Thin branches growing from the central leader as necessary to provide open space between limbs. Thin also some branches coming from these limbs, and so on, to the outermost branches. Remove all small downward branches growing out of bigger limbs. Eventually you'll need to cut out the top of the tall central leader — that is, once it starts to sag under a load of heavy fruit, forming a canopy over part of the tree and shutting out needed light.

central leader

Modified central leader

WHY: This method is easier than central leader because most fruit trees grow this way naturally. It ensures that fruit loads at the treetop are never as heavy as those at the bottom, where limbs are larger.

HOW: The modified-leader method is initially the same as the central-leader method, but over time you let the central trunk branch to form several tops. Reduce the tops of tall-growing trees from time to time to shorten the trees and to let in more light.

modified leader

Open center

WHY: This method lets more light into the shady interior of a tree. It produces trees with weaker branch structures than the previous methods create.

HOW: Prune so that the limbs forming the vase do not come out of the main trunk close to each other, or they will form a cluster of weak crotches. Even with the whole center of the tree open, you'll need to thin the branches and remove the older limbs eventually, just as you would with a tree pruned by the central-leader method.

open center

Q I ordered a dwarf apple tree online. Will it need special pruning at planting time?

A Probably not. Mail-order plants are usually sold bare-root for dormant planting, and these are typically top-pruned before shipping. Because bare-root fruit trees may be dug mechanically, they can sustain some root damage in the process. Pruning roots back to healthy tissue helps them heal smoothly.

If you've purchased a whip — a young fruit tree with no or weak side branches — plant it, cut it back to 30 to 36 inches high, and cut off any weak branches. Always prune to ¼ inch above a healthy bud.

cut back unbranched whips to 30 to 36 inches

prune broken roots

Hints for Success

Most fruit tree failures are due to improper planting rather than not pruning properly at planting time. Don't neglect the other steps in proper planting:

◆ Soak roots for several hours after arrival

◆ Soak ground well after planting

◆ Plant at the right depth, keeping the bud union 2 to 3 inches above ground

◆ Water regularly throughout the first year

Q Do I need to stake a newly planted fruit tree?

A Most trees won't need staking, but if your tree will grow on an open, windy site, set a 5- to 10-foot stake 2 feet in the ground roughly 4 inches from the trunk on the south side of the tree. Loosely tie the tree above the first set of branches to the stake with twine or flexible plastic tape.

Q I just planted two bare-root dwarf pears and two bare-root semidwarf apples. How do I start to train them?

A Pruning a new, bare-root fruit tree to have sturdy branches that can bear the weight of fruit begins in its first year. Apple and pear trees are initially pruned to a central leader (although that may change with age). After the tree starts growing, choose the strongest shoot to train as the leader or trunk. Pinch off competing shoots right below it, and choose four equally placed scaffolds about 6 to 8 inches apart. Because wide branch angles are important to tree strength and productivity, start training narrow branch angles by spreading with clothespins attached to the trunk above the shoot. Keep low limbs until tree is more established.

Q Do I have to keep training a semidwarf apple tree after the first year?

A Yes. In your tree's second year, keep widening narrow crotches. Snip off branches 18 inches or less from the ground. In early spring, encourage a strong leader by pruning out or cutting back vertical shoots competing with the leader. Cut back the leader by about one-third to force a second, higher layer of scaffold branches to emerge. Thin out some of the side branches (laterals)

year two

and shorten scaffolds, creating a sturdy structure for the tree. Lower scaffolds should be longer than upper ones. Keep limbs evenly spaced around the tree and at regular vertical intervals on the trunk, making sure that no two limbs emerge at the same height or place. If you were a bird flying over the tree, it would look like a wheel with the leader at the hub and eight spokelike, crooked branches around it.

Q I've been training my pears to a central leader for the past two years. Is there much training left to do?

A In the third year, prune off competing leaders. Pruning branches before bearing spurs are established delays fruiting. Remove water sprouts — vertical shoots from limbs — and suckers, especially those growing below the bud union, to keep up the tree's energy. For a third level of scaffold branches, head back the leader another time. Also take off all fruit on the leader.

In year four and beyond, continue removing side shoots that compete with the leader. Train a young, healthy central-leader fruit tree to have branches smaller on the tree top and wider on the bottom so maximum sunlight reaches them. Take off scaffold branches that grow too big and start to shade out the limbs below.

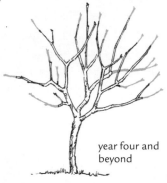

year four and beyond

229

Q What are spur-type fruit trees? How do I prune them?

A Trees bear their fruit either on the main limbs or on short, stubby branches called spurs, which grow off the limbs. Pears, plums, and cherries grow mostly on spurs (**A**). Peaches are borne on one-year-old limb growth and pomegranates at the tips of new growth (**B**). Most varieties of apples are produced on both spurs and on limbs.

Because spur-type fruit trees grow more slowly, they need less pruning. Because this means considerably less labor for the orchardist, scientists have bred trees that produce mostly on spurs, and many varieties are now available.

When too many fruit spurs develop along a branch, cut out some of them to encourage bigger and better fruits on the rest. This helps to reduce the amount of thinning you need to do each year. After a few years of experience, you'll be able to judge about how many spurs are right for your tree. Each spur usually produces for several years, after which time you should remove it so a replacement can grow. You'll be able to spot the older spurs because they get long and look spindly.

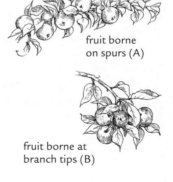

fruit borne on spurs (A)

fruit borne at branch tips (B)

Q My new plum tree is not supposed to grow very big. Why do I have to prune it?

A Since plums and cherries are apt to grow into a bushy form no matter what you do, early shaping is important mainly to keep them from getting too wide — and to prevent the branches from growing too close to the ground.

Q Our 'Red Delicious' apple tree has upright branches. Last year it looked weighed down by the fruit crop. Is it too late to shape the tree?

A Apples, pears, and peaches produce much heavier fruit loads than do plums and cherries. When growing apples and pears, you'll find that some need more shaping than others. Many apples, such as 'Wealthy' and 'McIntosh', seem to grow into a good shape quite naturally. Others, like 'Red Delicious' and 'Yellow Transparent', tend to grow very upright, forcing lots of tops with bad crotches. Prune upright-growing trees to get rid of weak crotches that are likely to break under a heavy load of fruit.

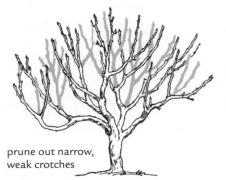

prune out narrow, weak crotches

Q How do I prune a dwarf Asian pear tree?

A Dwarf trees require some pruning just as full-sized trees do, but their height needs no control. Moreover, since they grow more slowly, they need pruning less often. You may want to thin some fruit to encourage trees to produce larger ones. Miniature fruit trees grown in tubs or planters for ornamental purposes also need some snipping back during the summer to keep them attractive.

Q I live in northern New England, where there's a ton of snow. Does that affect how I prune fruit trees?

A If you live in an area where snows are heavy and the average accumulation is around 3 feet, or if the snow drifts that high around the trees, eliminate branches near the ground. Heavy ice crusts sometimes settle as the snow underneath melts, breaking lower limbs in the process. This causes ugly wounds in a tree's trunk. Dwarf fruit trees may not be the best choice for you, because their branches are mostly low-growing.

Q I recently planted a five-in-one apple tree. What's the best way to prune it?

A As a novelty, some nurseries sell three-in-one or five-in-one apple trees, and a few even feature specimens with plums, cherries, peaches, nectarines, and apricots all growing on the same tree. Though they may be useful for a small growing area, these multiple-variety fruit trees are difficult to prune. If you have one, follow these tips:

◆ **Mark the varieties.** You will have to remember each year where the different varieties are located, or else you may cut off the only limb bearing a certain kind of fruit. If you don't have a good memory, tie ribbons of various colors to identify each one.

◆ **Grow your multiple-fruit tree with an open center** (see page 225), since there will be at least three strong limbs. Each kind of limb will grow at its own rate and in a different manner, so you'll need to do corrective pruning to produce a well-balanced tree. It's a big job. Keep at it to avoid bad crotches, water sprouts, and lopsided growth.

◆ **Be careful not to inadvertently remove branches you want to keep.** Take your time when pruning and examine the whole branch before making a cut. Unless you pay close attention to the task at hand, it's easy to prune off a grafted variety.

Q How should I prune my Damson plum tree to keep it healthy?

A Even a young tree occasionally needs to be pruned because of some mishap. Limbs break, tent caterpillars build nests, and branches die. As the tree gets older, rot and winter injury may take their toll on its branches.

Annual pruning makes fruit trees produce healthy new wood. This ongoing rejuvenation is vital to a tree's health, especially when your goal is to produce good crops of high-quality fruit over a number of years. Without this pruning, many trees that produce handsome specimens while they are young or middle-aged often bear only small, poor fruits as they grow older. By removing excess branches and letting sunlight penetrate the crown, you encourage the tree to bring forth large red apples or big crops of juicy plums or peaches.

prune out water sprouts and drooping branches

The apricot trees I planted a few years ago are now bearing fruit. How do I prune them to keep them producing well?

As with cars, regular tune-ups keep fruit trees going strong. You'll get the best results when you prune on an annual basis rather than as an occasional event.

◆ **Remove dead and damaged wood.** Clip or saw off the injured part back to a live limb or the trunk. Sick limbs will speed the decline of the tree.

- **Remove branches to thin out and open up** the tree to enable sunshine to reach and ripen the fruit. Thinning allows air to circulate, which discourages disease, and makes it easier for birds to pick up preying insects.
- **Remove a couple of the oldest limbs.** If you do this annually, the whole bearing surface can be renewed every six or eight years, which is like getting a whole new tree. In addition, this will minimize the need to do any drastic pruning of large, heavy limbs, and the tree will suffer less.
- **Cut off crossed branches** and any that might rub and cause wounds in the bark.
- **Remove water sprouts promptly.** These are upright, vigorous-growing branches that appear in clumps, often from a large pruning wound. They cause unwanted shade and are usually unproductive. (The more a branch tilts toward horizontal, the more fruit it bears.)
- **Remove surplus fruits** when your tree sets too many (see Thinning Fruit, below).

Thinning Fruit

Q My fruit trees produce mostly puny fruits. What's wrong?

A You need to thin the fruits before they mature. Thinning does for fruit what disbudding does for flowers. Because the remaining fruits grow bigger and better, you'll end up with more bushels of usable fruit than if you hadn't thinned at all. Most commercial growers thin their fruit in order to get the large specimens you see in stores.

Together with proper pruning, thinning helps your tree not only to produce larger fruit, but also to produce annually. Many fruit trees have a tendency to set a large crop every other year, and some produce well only every third year. The production of too many fruits (and therefore seeds) taxes a tree's strength. When a tree bears too many fruits in any one year, it often bears few, if any, the following year.

thinning apples

Q When should I thin the fruits on my trees?

A The best time to thin is after the natural fruit drop in early summer. Keep an eye on your trees, and whenever you see a lot of little fruits on the ground, give nature a helping hand by thinning the fruit still on the tree. Don't wait too long! Go out and remove excess fruits early in the season, while they're still tiny, so the tree doesn't invest its energy in them.

BEST CANDIDATES FOR THINNING

Thinning is good for a plant and good for you because it improves the size and quality of the remaining fruit. Remember that each variety of fruit has a built-in size limit, however, and no amount of disbudding or thinning will produce a fruit larger than that limit.

Thinning is usually less practical on trees with lots of small fruits, such as cherries, and most bush fruits, such as blueberries. On those, you can get some of the same benefit from pruning.

These fruits will benefit the most from thinning:

- ◆ Apples
- ◆ Nectarines
- ◆ Pears
- ◆ Apricots
- ◆ Peaches
- ◆ Plums

Q How much fruit should I remove when thinning a fruit tree?

A If there are more than two fruits in a cluster, leave the biggest and best one and pick off all the rest. Ideally leave about 6 inches between each fruit. Since this involves picking off 80 to 90 percent of the fruits, it's a big job.

thin to 6 inches apart

Even a light thinning will improve your crop. (Try leaving one branch alone to see what a difference thinning makes.) Regular pruning cuts down on the number of fruits produced, and therefore the time you need to spend thinning.

Solving Problems

Q We inherited some fruit trees that don't look very good. Is it too late to fix them?

A Corrective pruning can often come to the rescue of badly pruned trees. Below are some typical situations:

PROBLEM. The tree has a weak (narrow) crotch. It will collect water, begin to rot, and eventually split or break off at this point.

SOLUTION. Cut out one of the forks. The result will be a crooked leader, but that is a big improvement nevertheless, and later the crook will straighten out considerably.

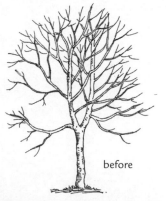

before

after

PROBLEM. The tree has several tops.
SOLUTION. Prune back to a single top. You may remove any remaining side branches later as the top grows taller.

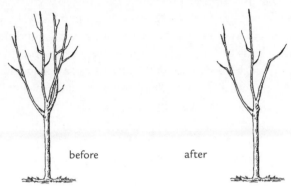

before   after

PROBLEM. The tree is tangled with growth.
SOLUTION. Simply removing all unnecessary growth may make a world of difference. Cut out dead, rubbing, and downward branches, branches that compete with each other, and those that have strayed too far from the rest of the tree.

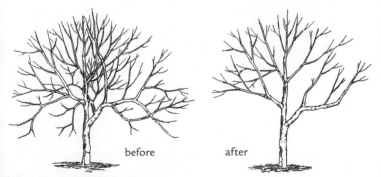

before   after

Q Our tree bore fruit soon after planting. Then it stopped. What happened?

A The time required by a young fruit tree to begin bearing is generally from 2 to 12 years, depending on the kind of fruit, the variety, the rootstock, and your growing conditions. When you buy a fruit tree, ask the nursery when you should safely expect the tree to bear. Don't let a tree bear fruit when it is too slight and immature. That weakens it, and it won't bear again for many years. It's difficult to say exactly when a tree is strong enough to bear its first crop; evaluate the strength of the limbs, the height, and its general health.

If you fear your tree is too small to mature fruits without weakening it, pick off the first blooms or small fruits. For example, if a semidwarf fruit tree blooms its second year, remove flowers before they can develop.

Q I have a fruit tree that has never produced fruit. What's wrong?

A Sometimes instead of bearing early in life, a tree does just the opposite. Some varieties, such as the 'Baldwin' apple and certain pears, take a long time to produce; others, in spite of careful pruning, are growing so luxuriously that they forget to settle down and bear fruit. Delayed bearing can result from root crowding or from weeds, lawn, and suckers growing around the base and sapping a tree's energy. Nonfruiting can also result from overly rich soil or not enough sunlight reaching the branches.

Try root pruning (see page 68) to slow down tree growth, which may get the tree to produce.

Q What are all the spindly branches growing from the base of my apple tree? What should I do about them?

A These are suckers, fast-growing shoots that are usually vertical and erect. They tend to appear as a cluster of branches close to the base of a tree trunk, but sometimes (especially on plums and cherries) they pop up from the roots anywhere under a tree, even a distance away from the trunk. Mow or clip them off at ground level as soon as they appear, while they're still on the small side and succulent.

suckers at the base of an apple tree

Q What causes suckers?

A A lot of sucker growth occurs on fruit trees when a slower-growing variety is grafted onto a vigorous-growing rootstock.

Q What's the difference between water sprouts and root suckers?

A Water sprouts emerge from branches; root suckers emerge from the ground.

water sprouts

Q What if I don't remove suckers and water sprouts?

A If they appear from below the graft, they'll grow into a wild tree or bush that will crowd out the good part of the tree within a few years. They will also sap valuable energy from the tree.

Q Can I transplant suckers?

A Because suckers look like new, young trees, it's tempting to think you can transplant them to form a new fruit tree of the same variety. But such trees usually produce fruit of inferior quality because they have come from the rootstock rather than the named variety.

Q Can I incorporate into my orchard seedlings that appear on the ground?

A In some unmowed orchards, trees sprout and grow from seeds of unused fruits that fall on the ground. Treat them like suckers and remove them as soon as they begin to grow. Like any weed, they sap energy from the orchard by depleting the water and fertility of the soil — and eventually they crowd out the good trees.

Although seedlings can often resemble the named varieties, their appearance is deceptive, and almost always the fruit is of inferior quality. Don't allow them, or any other weed, to compete with the vast root system your trees need to support the large crops of fruit you're anticipating.

Q What is sunscald?

A Sunscald is the most common type of winter injury to fruit trees. You'll recognize it if you see bark that looks sunken, discolored, or blistered and has small cracks or even large slits that run up and down the tree on the south or southwest side of the trunk.

Q What causes sunscald?

A Sunscald is traditionally considered a winter problem caused by a fast rise and fall in temperature. Affected cells on the trunk's southwest side break dormancy as direct sun heats the trunk. Frigid night temperatures kill the awakened cells. Sunscald can take place in any climate when bright, warm sun shines directly on a young tree's bark. It is especially hard on trees with little foliage to shade them. Particularly vulnerable are dark, thin-barked, moisture-stressed young trees that are either badly pruned or improperly planted, or suffered from root damage during transplanting. Freezing and thawing can also cause the trunk to expand and contract, cracking bark in the process.

Q What can I do to treat sunscald?

A With a clean, sharp knife, cut away dead bark to healthy tissue as soon as you see it. Let the opening heal without painting or treating it.

Q Can I prevent sunscald?

A Orchardists sometimes spray a thinned white latex paint on tree trunks every two or three years to reflect winter sun. This helps keep the tree sap cool. Whitewashing the tree stems is also useful in the South, where excessive sun often blisters the bark during hot summers. In areas where winter sunscald is predominant, you can also cover the trunk from the base to just above the bottom limbs with crepe-paper tree wrap. Do this in mid-fall and remove it right after the last frost in spring. Repeat this process each fall until the bark thickens, usually two or more years, depending upon the tree.

Q I pruned my fruit tree late last summer. Some new growth didn't survive winter. What happened?

A Sometimes a tree doesn't stop growing soon enough in late summer to harden up its new growth, which can't withstand the first cold spell or the extreme cold of winter. Or untimely late-winter thaws may stimulate bud activity, and the trees lose moisture that the frozen roots can't replace. The result is winterkill.

Q How can I keep winterkill from happening?

A Cut out damaged wood early in the spring. If the winter damage is severe, a heavy pruning of damaged wood will probably be all that the tree can stand, so don't do any additional pruning that year. (When this happens, don't fertilize for a year to prevent overstimulation of growth in an already weak tree.)

Sometimes it is difficult to tell which limbs are really dead and which are merely slow about leafing out. If in doubt, postpone the pruning for a few weeks, just to be sure.

In addition, follow these tips to reduce winterkill:

- ◆ **Choose varieties** that are suitable for growing in your region (that is, hardy in your USDA hardiness zone).
- ◆ **Prune carefully** and at the right time.
- ◆ **Fertilize only in spring and early summer,** so you don't stimulate late growth.
- ◆ **Before winter arrives,** cover tree roots with a heavy mulch of hay, shredded bark, or leaves so the ground doesn't freeze deep or warm up suddenly. This mulch will help to prevent root injury and also keep the tree from running out of moisture.

Q I neglected my small orchard for a while, and some of the trees are now excessively tall. What can I do?

A Ideally, you should prune regularly so that trees won't get too tall in the first place. At this point, however, you'd do well to remove some trees, though cutting down healthy trees just because you or someone else planted too many is a traumatic experience. Still, thinning the number of too-big trees is often the only way to achieve a good orchard.

When it comes to downsizing individual specimens, it's possible to improve the framework of a too-tall tree but it will take several years to accomplish. During that time you could plant a new dwarf or semidwarf apple tree that would begin to bear fruit in its third year.

Q How should I prune an ancient fruit tree that I really want to save?

A There is usually no way to get a sprawling, crotchy old tree back to growing with a model central leader without serious shock to the tree, and you can't top tall ones safely if they are past their prime. Usually, opening up a tree's center and thinning the wood for light and air are the only pruning you can hope to do on an elderly tree.

Q Can we salvage a decrepit orchard on our farm?

A Many folks ask the same question when faced with an old tree or orchard. Sometimes it is better to clear the land, stack up a big woodpile, and start over — but not always. Before you decide to try to save an old orchard, answer these two questions honestly:

◆ **Are the trees too far gone?** If their trunks are full of rot and large holes, or if they're half dead and splitting apart, they're probably on their last legs, and any pruning might finish them off.

- **Is the fruit that the trees produce any good?** If it is green, hard, sour, and small, the trees are probably of a poor variety. Perhaps they grew as suckers from the roots of other trees now gone, or from seeds that grew out of fallen, unused fruit. Unless the fruit is worth cooking or making into cider, it's just as well to get rid of such trees.

 Q How can I get a neglected orchard back in shape?

A If the trees look sound and the fruit looks like it could be improved with thinning, fertilizing, and pruning, then clean up the orchard and prune the trees. You can do this over the course of several years. If the trees are not in desperate condition, or if they respond well to the initial pruning, you may accelerate the process.

Here's what you do for starters:

- **With saw and scythe,** remove brush and weeds, trees other than fruit trees, and fruit trees that look decrepit or produce worthless fruit.
- **Remove loose bark** on remaining good trees, being careful not to open new wounds.
- **Cut off dead limbs and broken branches,** cutting each back to the branch collar without leaving a stub. Follow directions for cutting large branches (see

page 63) so that the wood doesn't split back into the trunk.

◆ **On trees that need severe pruning,** cut out limbs with woodpecker holes, weather damage, or signs of insect or disease infestation. That's enough for the first year. On trees requiring little pruning, begin removal of smaller limbs around the top of the tree to let in light. Don't cut too many live limbs in any year, unless their weight threatens the tree.

◆ **Haul away debris** — wood, bark, and brush — so insects and disease won't reproduce in it.

year one

Q What do I do after the first year?

A The following year, begin light pruning at the top of each tree so that more sunlight can reach the interior. Remove no more than one-quarter of a tree's limb area at one time. Less is better. Also cut out a few older, medium-sized, weak, and unproductive branches.

year two

The third year, thin out the branches even more. Start removing some larger branches to renew the tree. From then on, prune normally. If a tree appears to be in good physical condition, with many lower limbs and adequate new growth, begin to shorten the top. Your orchard, thanks to careful pruning, should now look better and begin producing a tasty crop.

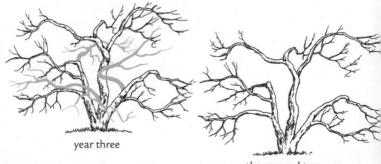

year three

the rescued tree

PRUNING SANITATION

Pruning tools can transmit serious diseases unless you keep them clean. For example, fire blight — a bacterium-caused disease that's lethal to fruit trees, especially pears — is spread around an orchard through tools.

If you suspect disease, think of yourself as a tree doctor when you prune. You wouldn't expect a surgeon to take out your gallbladder with the same dirty instruments she used to remove her last patient's appendix. Your tree deserves careful treatment with disinfected tools.

Disinfect your tools after pruning each tree. For home gardeners, it is safe and effective to soak the tools in a pail containing a household disinfectant such as Lysol or rubbing alcohol as you go between branches or trees. Just dip shears and saws into solution and wipe off the excess before making the next cut. With these germ-free tools, you can approach your trees with a clear conscience and do them no harm.

Tips for Specific Fruits

Q I grow several kinds of apple trees that vary somewhat in shape. Do I prune them all the same?

A To prune apple trees, follow the general directions in How to Shape Fruit Trees, page 224. Keep the tree growing with a central leader, if possible, and correct any bad growth habits common for your variety of tree.

Different apple varieties have somewhat different growth habits, so observe your tree and try to work with its natural tendencies. For example, 'McIntosh' is a nearly ideal tree, a strong, spreading grower with a naturally sturdy form. 'Red Delicious', on the other hand, will form many weak crotches if left alone; it is a dense grower, so you will need to thin out more branches. 'Cortland' has a spreading, somewhat drooping growth habit; don't allow branching too close to the ground. Prune 'Jonathan' heavily to correct its twiggy habit of growth. Some apples such as 'Empire' bear mostly on short spurs, so be careful not to damage these when pruning.

Q What's the best way to prune a cherry tree?

A Cherry trees (*Prunus cerasus, P. avium*) need less pruning than do other fruit trees.

♦ **Start pruning to a central leader** when your tree is young to encourage a strong tree, especially if it is one of the larger-growing types. Because of the tree's natural habit of growth, you will probably have to change to a modified leader or open center as it gets older.

◆ **You'll need to do some moderate pruning to let in sun** to color the fruit, and to thin out the bearing wood.

◆ **Beware of overpruning,** which can lead to winter injury and premature aging.

SEE ALSO: *How to Shape Fruit Trees, pages 224–225.*

Q Any tips on pruning citrus trees?

A Because oranges, grapefruits, lemons, and limes (*Citrus* spp.) grow in the hottest parts of the United States, they usually need less pruning than do fruit trees grown in the North, where pruning is needed to let sunlight into the trees. Over time, they develop a domed canopy. The wood is strong, and most trees produce crops inside the shaded crown. Remove water sprouts, suckers, and dead, broken, and diseased branches. If fruits stop forming inside the crown of an older tree, remove some interior branches for better light penetration. You can train citrus trees into fancy shapes, such as espaliers, cordons, and fences, if you do it with care. Dwarf varieties are usually best, and they can also be grown in large pots or planters.

Q The crown of my dwarf kumquat tree looks unbalanced. How and when can I prune it to look better?

A Sometimes citrus trees grow unevenly. If that bothers you, prune back the overlong limbs to a healthy, outfacing bud or branch. You can do this at any time of year, but in areas where frost is likely, wait until all danger of frost is past in the spring. Dwarf citrus need a lot less pruning than standard trees do.

Q How do I prune an old 'Meyer' lemon tree?

A Both dwarf and full-sized citrus trees may lose their vigor as they get older, so a rejuvenation pruning may be necessary to help them bear well again. Citrus trees can stand a more rigorous cutback than can peaches or apples, because winter injury is rarely a problem.

If you cut back a tree severely, clip and train new branches so the tree grows back into a good shape. It will probably take at least two years before it begins to bear well again. The hot summer sun can easily blister tender citrus bark, so be sure to whitewash any bark that you suddenly expose to the sun through heavy pruning. Also whitewash any bark exposed because of winter injury.

Q When and how do I prune a fig tree?

A Prune figs (*Ficus carica*) during their dormant season, cutting off dead and damaged wood. Figs grow from 10 to 30 feet tall and can stand heavy pruning, but once shaped, they really shouldn't need much pruning. Shrub thinning will cut back the early fruit crop but increase the main (second) crop, which occurs on new wood. Figs make good espaliers.

- **White and brown figs** bloom and bear only on new wood, so the usual practice is to cut these back severely each year for better production.
- **Prune black figs** more like other fruits, by cutting back wood that is over a year old.
- **Root pruning** is sometimes necessary to promote fruiting if they are growing in overfertile soil — in fact, fig trees do better where the soil isn't too rich.

Q How should I prune my peach and nectarine trees?

A The peach (*Prunus persica*) has always represented a real challenge to dedicated gardeners. It is fussy about soils and climate, sensitive to spring frosts, and grows so vigorously that heavy pruning is needed. Yet the juicy, tasty peach is so enticing that even Northerners keep trying to grow it. Those fortunate enough to live where the peach grows well naturally want to grow it to perfection. Proper pruning plays an important role in peach culture, and an unpruned tree is a sorry sight, bearing fruit only at the ends of saggy branches.

- **Grow both the peach and the nectarine with an open center.**
- **The trees tend to grow fast** and late in the season, and pruning makes them grow even faster. In areas where winter damage often kills improperly hardened wood, root pruning may be the only effective way to check excessive limb growth late in the season.
- **Don't allow peach and nectarine trees** to branch close to the ground, or you won't be able to keep trunk borers under control.
- **Even if you faithfully prune and thin,** peach trees tend to set such a heavy crop that broken branches are a danger. Help your tree by propping up weighty limbs with wide planks.

train to an open center

Q When's a good time to prune my peach tree?

A The best time to prune is on a dry day in late winter, so you can cut away wood injured by low temperatures. In years when winter damage is heavy, this pruning may be all the tree can stand. Otherwise, because fruiting occurs on one-year wood only, you can remove older wood. Never feed a tree after you've had heavy winter damage or pruned it severely; you don't want to stimulate rapid regrowth.

Like all fruit trees, peaches often set far too many little fruits — even when pruned well. To get large, luscious peaches, thin after normal fruit drop in early summer, spacing 6 or 7 inches apart. This may be tedious and time-consuming, but the results will be well worth your effort.

Q My nectarine tree is so tall that it's hard to harvest the fruit. Will I hurt the tree if I cut it back?

A Peach, nectarine, and apricot trees are likely to grow tall. Since the best fruit often grows at the top of the tree, keep the top low and accessible. The best method is to cut back the tall-growing limbs each year. If you haven't done this regularly, you can remove the top of the tree during the dormant season with no trauma to the tree. However, the fruit crop may be less the following year.

Q How do I prune apricot trees?

A Treat apricots (*Prunus armeniaca*) like peaches. Train to an open center. Prune heavily for the best crops and so the tree will bear annually. Remove branches to let sunlight reach the spurs, in order to produce good fruit. Spurs bear for about four years and need to be removed thereafter.

Some growers prefer to prune in summer because it results in less-vigorous regrowth. In some climates, it can also save the tree from the ill effects of pruning on wet winter days, when many disease fungi are active. Where the growing season is short, root pruning may help prevent excessive growth without subsequent winter injury.

Q I'd like to plant some pear trees. Are they difficult to grow?

A Pears (*Pyrus communis*) are not as difficult to grow as are peaches, but in past years fire blight killed off many trees. Fortunately for pear lovers, quite a few blight-resistant varieties have been introduced. An annual light pruning is better than an infrequent heavy one; heavy pruning delays bearing and encourages fire blight.

Like most fruits, pears need a partner for pollination, so always plant at least two varieties. Consider 'Moonglow' and 'Starking Delicious', which will pollinate each other and flourish in most pear-growing areas.

Q How do I prune my pear tree?

A Follow these tips:

◆ **The early training of pears** is similar to that of apples. Prune to a central leader for the first few years. After that, grow them with a modified leader, if you'd like.

◆ **The growth of most varieties tends to be upright,** so direct early pruning toward thinning excess branches and encouraging a spreading tree.

◆ **Many pear varieties grow with several tops,** so prune out extra tops to keep a strong central leader and to avoid narrow crotches that tend to break easily when loaded with fruit.

◆ **Pears bloom and bear on the short, sharp spurs** that grow between the branches. Spurs need regular thinning; occasionally remove older ones so vigorous young ones can replace them. Thin out the small fruits after the normal fruit drop in early summer.

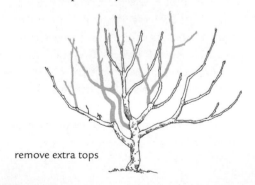

remove extra tops

Q What is fire blight?

A Fire blight is a contagious bacterial disease affecting pears, quince, apples, crab apples, and other members of the rose family. You can spot it easily because the limbs, leaves, and twigs look as if they have been held over a flame. Cut diseased limbs completely back into good, healthy wood. Remove them to a safe distance and burn, bury, or otherwise destroy them, so the disease doesn't spread. Sterilize your gloves and all tools in bleach solution after pruning each tree.

Always be on guard for signs of fire blight. Early detection is important so that you can bring it quickly under control.

Q How do I pick a plum tree for my garden?

A No matter where you live, there's a plum tree (*Prunus* spp.) for you. Choose one suited to your climate and desired color — red, blue, yellow, purple, and green plums are available in a wide range of sizes and flavors. Some are self-fruitful; others require two varieties for pollination. European varieties (*P. domestica*), some hardy up to –50°F, are best for cold climates with late frosts; Japanese plums (*P. salicina*) thrive in warmer zones. Little wild European plums (*P. insititia*) such as Mirabelles and damsons are another option, along with American plum (*P. americana*), a thorny shrub or small tree hardy to USDA Zone 3.

One-year-old whips, from 4 to 7 feet tall, are the best choice if you are planting European or American plums, and two-year-old, slightly branched trees are preferable if you are planting the Japanese varieties. Cut back the whips by about one-third to a fat bud.

Q How do I prune an established plum tree?

A Prune your plum tree carefully to help it produce well and to allow the sun to ripen the fruit before the first frost hits. Due to the scraggly habit of growth, plums are best grown with an open center. Thin out water sprouts and inside branches to allow sun penetration and to keep up fruit production inside the tree.

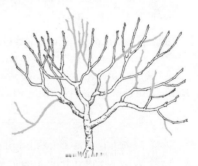

Q When should I prune my plum?

A It depends on the type of plum you're growing:

♦ **Japanese plums** are vigorous and require a lot of pruning, which you should do annually in late winter.

- **European plums** need very little; an occasional thinning of older wood is usually all that is necessary.
- **Most American plums** and their hybrids need only moderate pruning to keep them bearing well. Some varieties, including some of the cherry–plum hybrids, grow very long branches that hang on the ground; these should be shortened.
- **Many plum roots** sucker badly, so periodically remove suckers unless you mow under the tree regularly.

Q Since plum fruits are relatively small, do I still need to thin the crop?

A Trees that produce large plums, such as the Japanese varieties, benefit from thinning. For best results, pick off the extra fruits when they are still tiny, in early summer, so that the remaining plums are 5 inches apart.

Q My plum tree bears huge crops every other year. Why won't it fruit every year?

A If your plum tree fruits heavily every other year, thin out some fruit to limit the crop, increase fruit size, and encourage annual bearing.

Q Do I need to worry about diseases with plums?

A Some plums, especially European varieties, are quite susceptible to a disease called black knot. Thick outgrowths form along the twigs and are particularly noticeable in winter. No spray is available to control black knot, so prune out all diseased material in winter, cutting 6 to 8 inches below a knot. Disinfect tools as you work. Burn or dispose of diseased parts promptly to prevent spreading the trouble. It's a good idea to remove infected wild plums or cherries growing nearby.

Q I just planted a quince tree for making jelly. Do I have to prune it?

A Quince (*Cydonia oblonga,* not flowering quince, *Chaenomeles*) is one of the few fruit trees that need almost no pruning, except to remove any broken, dead, diseased, injured, or crossed branches. Shape to get the tree growing into a good form; remove low branches that could touch the ground if weighed down by heavy fruits. Thin out limbs only if harvesting the fruit is difficult.

Like pears, quince trees are extremely susceptible to fire blight (see page 260).

thin too-dense limbs on a quince tree

263

TIPS FOR TROPICALS

PLANT	CHARACTERISTICS	MAINTENANCE
Avocado (*Persea* spp.)	Dense evergreen with glossy leaves	In tropical climates, opening up the tree causes sunscald on tender bark, so almost never pruned. For fruit: Allow tree to grow naturally.
Mango (*Mangifera indica*)	Long-lived tree with shiny evergreen foliage	In South: No special care outdoors. In North: Grow as pot plant; pinch back and root-prune (see page 68) occasionally to keep from growing too large; repot from time to time. Grow in ordinary garden soil; keep moist but not wet. Be careful with clippings, which can cause a severe rash, and do not burn.
Olive (*Olea europaea*)	Gnarly evergreen with grayish leaves	Needs heavy pruning; remove basal suckers frequently, also the occasional older branch. Usually grown as a tree but may be pruned to a shrub or tall, thick, hedge. If pruned carefully, can continue producing to a ripe old age. Fruits on last year's growth; removing some blooms helps trees bear each year.

PLANT	CHARACTERISTICS	MAINTENANCE
Papaya (*Carica papaya*)	Resembles a large perennial more than a tree; tends to grow tall, with no lower branches	Grow only where frosts are unlikely, or in a greenhouse. Pruning isn't necessary, but clipping the top in early spring promotes more than one trunk and greater productivity. For better appearance, remove the old brown and yellow leaves that often hang on the tree during winter.
Pomegranate (*Punica granatum*)	An ornamental tree that grows to an attractive shape with little care	For food production, grow in tree form and remove all suckers. As an ornamental, can train as an espalier (see page 179).

 How do I grow tropical and semitropical fruits?

Only gardeners in completely frost-free regions can safely grow tropical fruits outdoors. Elsewhere, you can grow them in a heated greenhouse or a conservatory.

What is grafting?

Grafting is not a mysterious operation, and almost any good fruit-growing book or website will show you how it's done. Basically, you take a branch from a tree that bears good fruit and surgically transplant it to the root of a wild or unimproved tree. Bud grafting is similar except that you use a single dormant bud. Grafting is useful to create varieties that nurseries don't sell, and to propagate choice old varieties that are nearly obsolete.

CHAPTER 12

Pruning Bush Fruits, Brambles, and Grapes

Much of your family's best winter eating can come from the berry patch. Each year you can stock your freezer with raspberries, blueberries, currants, gooseberries, and elderberries. By late fall, jars of preserves and colorful juices will line your pantry shelves, ready to eat through winter. These small fruits come in many hues, flavors, shapes, and sizes. There are red, pink, and green varieties of gooseberries; black, purple, red, and pink raspberries; and many different grapes, blueberries, blackberries, and currants.

Bush fruits, brambles, and grapes are tasty, full of vitamins, and easy to grow. They are productive — most bear a year or two after planting. The plants are usually inexpensive, need surprisingly little care, and take up very little room in the garden.

Prune bush fruits for the same reasons you prune fruit trees. Proper pruning extends the useful life of a berry patch by many years. Prune your grapes and berries well, and you will help them resist disease, produce larger fruit and better crops, and improve the harvest.

Grapes

Q Why should I prune my grapevines?

A You must prune grapes (*Vitis* spp.) to get good crops. Many varieties are rank growers; an unpruned plant can spread quickly over a large area, forcing its energy into the vine rather than into the production of grapes.

Grapes grow mostly on one-year-old wood (canes). As an unpruned vine matures, it carries more and more wood that is much older and thus becomes not only tangled but unproductive as well.

Q How do I go about it?

A Allow the canes to grow one year and bear fruit the next, then prune them off. Each summer your plant should have canes at two stages of growth: canes that grew last year and are now bearing and new canes that will bear next year.

Grape-pruning methods vary because different varieties grow at different rates and the pruning must be adjusted accordingly. Pruning also varies with soils and climates.

Keep in mind the following when pruning grapes:

- Prune to keep the vine to a manageable size.
- Prune to direct the energy of the vine into producing fruit rather than stems and leaves, and to keep the crop growing close to the main stem so that the sap doesn't have to travel far to produce grapes.

◆ Prune to let in sunlight so the fruit can ripen. Grapes must ripen on the vine because, unlike most other fruits, they do not continue to ripen after they are picked.

Q Do I need to prune grapes when I plant them?

A Because pruning at planting time is so important to a grapevine's future success, most nurseries prune the vines before they sell them. Ask the nursery if vines are pruned and ready to plant. If not, do it yourself, unless the vine is potted with its roots intact. You must steel yourself and prune heavily, so the roots will grow faster than the top and stimulate the vine to get off to a strong start. It will begin bearing heavy crops in two or three years.

1. Prune away all side branches.
2. Cut back the main stem to two or three buds, so that it is no more than 5 inches tall.

Q Do bush fruits and grapes need pruning?

A Yes. Although wild and neglected bushes and vines bear without pruning, you'll get better, more abundant crops if you prune regularly. Also, pruning makes it easier to pick the fruit. Proper pruning extends the useful life.

Pruning methods for bush fruits, brambles, and grapes are somewhat different.

Q When should I prune my grapevine?

A Always prune when your vine is dormant — anytime after the leaves drop in the fall but before the buds begin to swell in the spring, provided the temperature is above freezing. Most northern gardeners choose early-spring pruning so they can cut off winter injury at the same time.

Q I want to plant a grapevine. What are my growing options?

A You have several options, depending upon your goal:

◆ **On an arbor.** This way, you can enjoy the beauty of the vines while watching the ripening grapes hang from overhead.
◆ **On a trellis.** This enables you to espalier the vines against a wall or a building.

- **Over a fence.** A casual look that softens a fence's lines will provide you with a tasty, easy-to-reach harvest.
- **The Kniffen system.** This type of fence is meant to be highly practical and is not for show. However, grapevines grown in this way are easier to care for and most likely to be healthy and productive. (See Kniffen system, page 272.)
- **As freestanding plants.** Some gardeners, especially wine producers, like to prune their vines so that they have a single, long, tall trunk, like a cordon. Each year after fruiting, they cut back all the canes almost to this trunk, leaving a few short stubs to bear fruit and from which the new canes appear.

Q I'm planting grapes to grow over an arbor. How should I prune the vines?

A Again, your pruning depends upon your goal:

ORNAMENTAL. If you want a thick, shady vine with a few grapes hanging on it for effect, prune only to keep it from becoming overgrown.

ORNAMENTAL AND PRODUCTIVE. If you want grapes as well as beauty, prune annually to get rid of all wood over one year old. Cut back part of the year-old wood too, leaving only enough to cover the arbor and produce grapes the following year.

Q What's the easiest way to grow grapes? We don't want fancy trellises, just a reliable way to grow healthy grapes to eat.

A One of the easiest and best ways to care for grapes is the Kniffen system. Begin by choosing a good site. Your vines need as much sun as possible and as little of the chilling north wind as you can manage.

Each year, thin fruit clusters whenever too many appear. Usually a healthy, vigorous vine will produce from 30 to 60 bunches a year, with an average of 8 to 15 per branch. Don't allow the plant to produce a greater number, because overproduction weakens the vine, and you'll get quantity rather than quality.

The Kniffen system for grapes

Q What's the best support for growing grapes?

A You need a sturdy fence for the Kniffen system. Install two strands of smooth 9- or 10-gauge wire, stapled on posts set solidly in the ground and spaced about 8 feet apart. Space the lower wire about 3 feet above the ground and the second about 2 feet higher (**1**). Brace posts at their ends so wires won't sag when loaded with fruit and vines (**2**). Plant each grapevine midway between the posts (**3**).

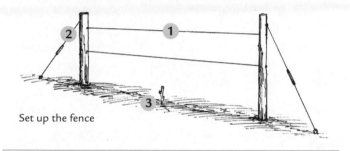

Set up the fence

Q How do I start with the Kniffen system?

A Implement this method as follows:

1. **After the initial cutting back at planting time** (see page 269), during the first summer allow vines to grow naturally. Remove side sprouts so vines grow upward toward the wires.

year one

2. **During the second summer,** by pinching and pruning, allow two vines to grow along the wires in each direction — four in all. If the vines grow well, they should cover the wires by summer's end (if they grow more, cut back extra growth and side branches 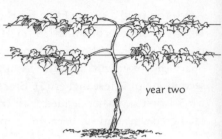 after the first hard frost). Grape tendrils should wrap around wires and hold vines securely. If any need to be reattached, use narrow plastic ribbon (not tape), which won't cut into tender bark.

year two

Q How do I prune once my grapes start bearing?

A The third year is your first bearing year! Let four more new vines grow parallel to those of the previous season. These newcomers replace ones that grew the second year. Let these droop on the ground until you cut off the old vines and are ready to fasten replacements to the wires.

Meanwhile, year-old vines should bloom and set grapes all along the wires this summer. Don't allow too many bunches to form, because overbearing weakens the plant and jeopardizes future crops. Remove some clusters of tiny grapes if more than three or four bunches form per vine. Continue to pinch back new growth headed in the wrong direction all season. Four new canes are all you'll need.

In late winter or early spring, cut off the four fruiting canes from the previous year. Make sure that you secure four new canes to the wires. These replace last year's bearing vines and produce this year's crop. Cut off extra growth, and during summer, pinch new canes occasionally to train four more canes that will replace those presently bearing. Repeat this process every year.

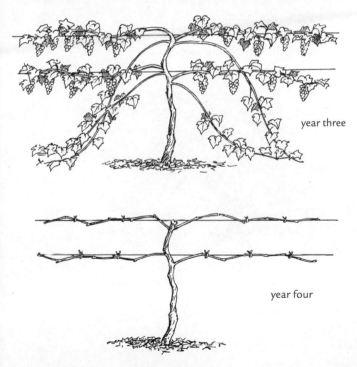

year three

year four

Q How do I go about rejuvenating a neglected grapevine?

A If the vine is badly overgrown, spread out the work over several years with the idea firmly in mind that you will eventually get the vine back to a single trunk with only four strong, well-spaced branches. Then you can train it into a Kniffen or other manageable system. Have a truck standing by to haul away the prunings, or plan a brisk bonfire in a safe place, because you'll have to get rid of lots of dead wood.

Try the following steps:

1. When the vine is dormant, choose a main trunk and remove all competing stems.

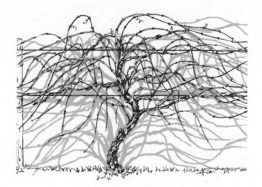

2. Choose two canes on each side (this year's growth) and flag them. These will be the bearing canes for this season.

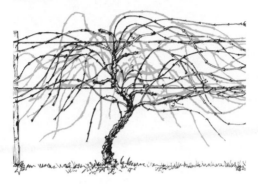

3. Cut back two more canes on each side, leaving two buds on each. These spurs will produce the bearing canes for the following year.

4. Prune out everything except the flagged canes and the spurs. Shorten the flagged canes to about 10 fruit buds each for best productivity, and tie them loosely to the wires.

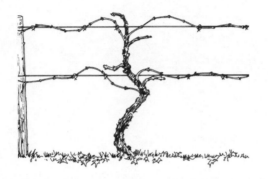

Q Parts of an old grapevine have taken root. Can I make new plants from the rooted pieces?

A Vines that trail over the ground for many years often root and form many new plants, which can be salvaged. In early spring, cut them back to about a foot. Then dig them up with a ball of soil and replant them where you please.

If you don't need or want new plants, cut off all rooted vines at ground level and don't allow them to grow back. Mow or spread heavy mulch over the area to control any regrowth.

Blueberries and Other Bush Fruits

Q Do bush fruits need much pruning?

A Bush fruits such as currants, elderberries, gooseberries, blueberries, and cranberries are not nearly as demanding as the tree fruits, brambles, or grapevines, which need annual upkeep. Some old farmsteads have currant and gooseberry bushes that produce large crops of excellent fruit after decades of neglect. They are resistant to most diseases and insects and, with the exception of blueberries, not at all fussy about soil. Each bush produces better with a little care, including pruning.

Q Should I prune a blueberry bush before planting?

A Plants in containers or growing with a well-wrapped and undisturbed ball of earth don't need pruning for the first few years, except to remove dead or damaged branches. Treat a bare-root fruit bush just as you would any low-growing shrub. Cut off any dead or damaged roots or branches. Also remove any crossed or rubbing branches.

Q How should I prune blueberry bushes for lots of fruit?

A Compared to other bush fruits, highbush blueberry (*Vaccinium corymbosum*) is a slow grower, taking as long as a decade to come into full production. So that you won't delay bearing, avoid pruning for the first three years, except to remove dead or broken limbs.

Blueberries tend to grow in a bushy manner with lots of small twigs. As a plant gets older, the twigs get thicker and bear less fruit. Follow these steps to keep mature bushes bearing abundant crops:

1. Cut two or three of the older main stems right back to the ground. Also remove any dead branches.

2. Thin out about half of the end twigs from the remaining branches to stimulate the plant to bear more heavily. Ideally, the pruned plant will have canes growing tighter at the base than at the top, which should be fairly open and without crossing stems.

REGIONAL BLUEBERRY PRUNING

Blueberries can be grown almost anywhere the weather is not too extreme. They do require acidic soil (pH of 4.5 to 5), so amend the chosen spot at planting time if necessary. And choose a variety that is known to do well in your climate. There are dozens to choose from, especially in specialty nursery catalogs.

IN MILD CLIMATES. As with many other fruits, blueberries grown in areas where the winter is mild should be pruned heavily. You can do this any time from when the leaves come off in the fall to the time that growth starts in very early spring.

IN COLD CLIMATES. If you have a short growing season and a cold winter, prune lightly each year, experimenting until you find what amount seems most beneficial to the plant. Do this in early spring, so you can remove any wood that was injured during the winter at the same time. Overfeeding and overpruning may induce winter injury and severely limit your crop. Be careful never to prune frozen wood, because your cut won't seal easily, resulting in additional winter injury to the plant.

LOWBUSH BLUEBERRY

This little, three-season shrub grows wild in New England, making a dense ground cover with bell-shaped white spring flowers, sweet edible summer fruits, and red fall color. The tiny, frosty blue fruits are sweet, meaty, yummy, and better for baking than highbush blueberries, which are more watery.

Q What fruit can I grow that doesn't need pruning every year?

A Try currants or gooseberries. Abandoned plants often continue to produce good crops for decades, although the fruit is small. Even a little pruning will improve yields, however.

For the best yields of currants and gooseberries, a little pruning pays off. Begin to thin out your bush when it is about three years old. Stems that are older than that bear poorly and should be cut off at ground level or as close to the soil as possible. New, vigorous growth will quickly replace them. To produce its best, a currant or gooseberry bush should have wood that is one to three years old, and little or none that is any older.

SEE ALSO: *Pages 285–286 for elderberries.*

Q I've had my gooseberry bushes for two years. Do they need regular pruning?

A Usually the initial pruning will be all your bush needs for several years. Cut off any dead twigs or branches and those that have been broken by weather or birds. Otherwise, just let the bush grow.

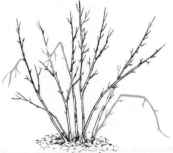

Q Can pruning help my currants produce bigger berries?

A Yes. After your bush has borne several large crops of fruit, you may notice that it looks a bit overgrown and that the fruits are getting smaller. It's time to thin it out. Select a few of the oldest branches and cut them right to the ground, either in late fall or in early spring. If you do this faithfully every few years, the bush should continue to produce and thrive.

Q Do currants and gooseberries perform well in the South?

A Currants and gooseberries (*Ribes* spp.) are cool-weather plants, grown in northern areas. Although new varieties are being developed for the South, these fine bush fruits grow best where summers are cool and winters are cold.

Q The fruits on my gooseberry bushes seem to be shrinking in size. What's wrong?

A With heavier pruning, you can force giant-sized gooseberry varieties to produce fruit as large as grapes or small plums. Thin out the berries as soon as they form. Pick off the tiniest berries and leave the remaining ones about 1 inch apart on the branch. (With thorny varieties, however, this process may not be an entirely pleasant task, or worth the trouble.)

Q Can I make old currant bushes more productive?

A If you have a neglected bush, give it a new lease on life by cutting it off at ground level and letting a new plant grow back. Doing all this in one year would be hard on even a vigorous plant, so spread out the job over at least a couple of years.

◆ In very early spring, before any green shows, cut off about half of the old stems at ground level, leaving any young, lively ones. That year, you should see a lot of new growth.

◆ The next year, cut the remaining old stems to the ground. These, too, will regrow, and you will have a completely new plant that you'll be proud to show off, and one that will be easier to prune and care for in the usual manner.

Q I intend to buy an elderberry for my backyard. Does it require much pruning?

A Both wild and garden elderberries (*Sambucus* spp.) are a fine addition to anyone's backyard berry patch. Elderberry is a wonderful fruit, and I'd hate to be without it. However, plants are tall (to 7 feet) and extremely vigorous growers. Grow them only where you can keep them safely under control by mowing around them regularly. They grow well only in moist areas, and you should never plant them near a vegetable garden, flower bed, or other berries or plants.

Because they are so productive and robust, and since all the improved varieties have only recently emerged from the wild, elderberry plants need minimal pruning to keep them productive.

Q I love my elderberry! How can I keep it neat and bushy instead of tall and lanky like the ones by the side of the road?

A During the first summer, pinch off the top of the young plants to encourage side branching and earlier bearing. (Unlike the other bush fruits, early bearing won't hurt an elderberry plant at all.) Cut out any wood that gets broken during the winter, and remove old, corky stalks that no longer produce well. Mow or prune off the sucker plants that continually try to grow outside the clump. You can prune elderberries anytime, since they are such vigorous growers.

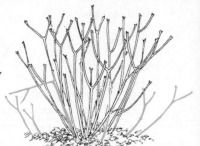

remove suckers and broken branches

Raspberries and Other Brambles

Q I want to grow raspberries and blackberries. What do I need to know?

A Raspberry and blackberry plants and their dozens of cousins — including the boysenberry, dewberry, youngberry, and marionberry — are usually referred to as the brambles (*Rubus* spp.). Unlike the bush fruits, which are really small trees, the brambles are woody biennials — actually, their canes are woody biennials. The roots are perennial, and under the right conditions, brambles will live for decades, perhaps even for centuries.

Here's how they grow: Each cane sprouts from the roots and grows to its full height in a season. The following year it blooms, produces fruit, and dies that same season. (Everbearing raspberries follow a slightly different

cutting out old canes after fruiting is essential

routine; see page 290.) At the same time, other canes are growing that will produce their fruit the following year. And so the patch marches on.

Cutting out old canes after fruiting is central to bramble-fruit culture. An old frugal Yankee once said that he "warn't goin' to cut nothin'" out of his patch, because there was always a chance that dead canes might bear something another year. In about three years, he had a jungle of dead canes and almost no fruit — his patch had killed itself by overpopulation. Anyone who enjoys wild-berry picking has seen this happen to an uncultivated patch — in a few years, there are no plants left. There is a reason: Nature arranged it so that brambles are an interim crop, holding their own until trees get a foothold. Pruning, however, can make a difference.

Q Should I prune brambles the first year I plant them?

A You don't have to cut back the tops, except for damaged stems. If you bought them in pots, untangle any encircling roots. For bare-root shrubs, prune off broken roots.

Q What's the best way to grow brambles?

A Set the plants 24 to 36 inches apart in a straight row. If you plant more than one row, keep the rows at least 6 feet apart. While this may seem like wasted space, berry plants are such virile growers that they soon make a wide row. Unless you leave adequate space, you'll have no room to walk between the rows. Also, by spacing them correctly, you won't have to cut out a lot of thorny growth. Place bare-root blackberries and raspberries 1 inch deeper in the soil than they grew at the nursery. Check the dark soil line near the roots to determine how deep they were previously buried.

Support mature plants with double rows of smooth wire on each side of the row.

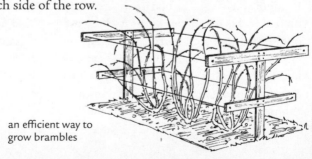

an efficient way to
grow brambles

288

Q How do I prune raspberries and upright blackberries?

A In late summer after you have picked the berries, remove old, dying canes that produced fruit this year by cutting to the ground. Remove (or mow over) any plants coming up between the rows. Before winter, also:

◆ Cut out small, weak canes at ground level to divert the plant's energy into the main stems.

◆ Thin strong canes so they are at least 5 or 6 inches apart.

◆ Cut back the remaining canes to about 5 feet in height to make them stiff enough to stand upright over the winter without support.

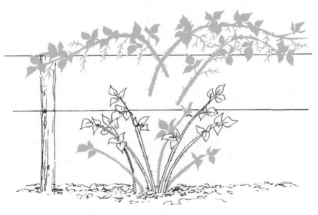

cut out weak canes and
thin strong canes

Q I just bought some everbearing raspberries. How should I prune them?

A Several varieties of red and yellow raspberry plants are sold as "everbearers." They do not produce constantly throughout the summer, as the name implies, but they do bear a crop in midsummer on one-year-old canes (as do most raspberries) plus another, usually smaller, crop in the fall on the new canes that have just finished growing.

If you have only one kind of raspberry and it is an everbearer, you can treat it just as you do the regular bearers. Cut out the old canes just after they finish bearing their summer crop, then harvest a fall crop off the new canes, leaving them to produce again the following summer.

However, many gardeners who have both regular and everbearing varieties prefer to skip the summer crop on the latter to harvest a bigger fall crop. They do this by treating the raspberry canes as annuals, cutting them to the ground right after the fall crop is harvested. Since there are never any one-year-old canes, there is never any summer crop the following year. The fall harvest is not only larger but earlier as well, since all the plant's energy goes into it. There's only one thing as tasty as a fresh raspberry in season, and that's a fresh raspberry out of season.

Q What should I do with all the little blackberry plants that formed last summer where the ends of long trailing canes curved down and touched the ground?

A Purple and black raspberries and trailing blackberries form new plants by a process known as tipping. In late summer, their long canes bend over until the ends touch the soil; roots then grow at these tips and a new plant is born. Keep them under constant control, just as with suckers.

Q I want to plant only one bush. Do I need a fancy support?

A If you have only one bush, try tying the branches to a post. That should be sufficient.

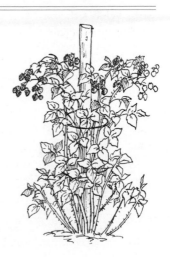

Q I'm finding my raspberries hard to control. How can I keep their suckers from taking over my small garden?

A The large root systems of red and yellow raspberries and upright-growing blackberries send up lots of suckers, which sometimes appear several feet away from the row. Always cut them off at ground level. Mulch generously, and mow or cultivate between the rows.

Q What's the best way to grow vine-type brambles like boysenberries?

A Vinelike blackberries and the closely related dewberries, boysenberries, and youngberries grow taller than other brambles. Fasten them to wires about 5 feet high supported by posts. Allow three or four strong canes to grow from each plant and thin out the others. Allow those that grew the previous season to bear fruit and another set to grow as replacements to produce the following year's crop. Cut out the old canes soon after you harvest the berries. The following year, fasten the new canes to the wires. Grow black and most purple raspberries the same way.

Q I'm starting over because my bramble patch became a jungle. Any tips?

A Every summer, without fail, cut out old canes as soon as they finish bearing. You can identify them by their appearance: they are tan or brown and tend to be woody, in contrast to the new canes, which are young and green.

Thin out the new canes to allow better air circulation and reduce the chances of mildew, spur blight, and other diseases. Thinning also results in larger berries. First, cut out all weak, small, short, and spindly canes. Then thin the healthy, large canes so that the remaining ones are 6 inches apart.

Cut back tall-growing brambles to about 5 feet, but short-growing varieties need only a few inches snipped off. Pruned canes tend to stand winter winds and snows without breaking and are better able to hold up the following year's fruit without flopping to the ground.

Burn old canes or get them out of the neighborhood as fast as possible. Never use the canes as mulch or put them in the compost pile, because they rot slowly and may be harboring harmful insects or diseases.

Q Can pruning help keep my brambles healthy and free from pests and diseases?

A Check your patch often throughout the summer to see that diseases and insects haven't launched an assault. The two most common maladies are both easily treatable by timely pruning:

SYMPTOM. Whole canes wilt and die.

CULPRIT. Spur blight, a common disease of bramble fruits, is infecting your plants.

TREATMENT. Prune out and burn or bury all the dying canes as soon as you notice them.

SYMPTOMS. In early summer, some of the top leaves on the new canes have wilted and the tops are drooping.

CULPRIT. The cane borer. Look for two parallel rows of dots just below the wilted portion; a cane borer has deposited an egg right between the two circles.

TREATMENT. Cut off the top of the cane 6 inches below the lower circle and burn it, egg and all. If you don't, the resulting grub will live up to its name by boring down the cane and wrecking it. Then, down near the roots, the grub will develop into a clear-winged moth that will fly about your berry patch some night spreading more eggs and mischief.

SEE ALSO: *When Galls Are Not Harmless, page 85.*

CHAPTER 13

Pruning Nut Trees

Almonds, hazelnuts, pecans, and walnuts contribute to heart health because they're low in saturated fat and high in mono- and polyunsaturated fats. Nuts are also packed with nutrients including fiber, zinc, protein, magnesium, and phosphorus. Thus more people are racing squirrels to nut trees each fall and finding ways to keep their attics and garages squirrel-proof, so that they can store their nut caches safely.

Most nut trees grow far too big for a small backyard, but some make satisfactory shade trees. The demand for homegrown nuts has spurred a search for better strains, and growers continue to develop new varieties of bigger, better-flavored, and easier-to-crack nuts.

Commercial growers have planted nuts like the walnut, filbert, pecan, and almond for centuries. As a result, these nuts have the most named varieties in cultivation. Only in recent years has a serious attempt been made to improve black walnut, butternut, hickory, and chestnut trees. Beech trees have been developed that produce larger nuts. Research has produced trees that are more disease resistant and some that are suited to growing in areas where previously nuts could not be grown.

Should I prune a nut tree when I plant it?

A If you buy a container-grown nut tree, it won't need pruning at planting time; just untangle its roots. Bare-root trees were probably pruned before shipping, so prune only broken roots. If you must, shorten overly long roots, but leave the taproot as long as possible.

SEE ALSO: *Planting Trees, page 78.*

Q **When should I prune a nut tree?**

A Always do major pruning when the tree is dormant. Nut trees in a forest tend to grow straight and tall. Their lower limbs gradually die as the trees reach higher for the sun. In the open, many varieties of large nut trees spread out, and their limbs grow oddly. Sometimes the limbs grow straight up, forming a second top, or they may grow straight out.

Q **Should I treat nut trees as shade trees or fruit trees when I prune them?**

A That depends on the trees you choose, their natural habit, your location, and their usage in your yard. If you're growing a small nut tree such as an almond, prune it much as you would a fruit tree (see How to Shape Fruit Trees, pages 224–225). Easterners prune the filbert into a large bush; on the West Coast folks prune it as a small tree.

Most nuts, such as pecans and walnuts, grow on large trees. If you inherit one that's full-grown, treat it the same as a mature shade tree. If you plant a new one, train it to grow with a strong central leader (see Training Shade Trees, page 80). Sooner or later, you will have to give up and let the tree grow as crotchy and limby as it wants, but keep after it for as long as you can.

Q I have some wonderful old nut trees that shade my house all summer. Can I prune them without ruining their canopies?

A Prune large nut trees for the same reason that you would prune a shade tree — to remove dead or injured limbs. Prune off limbs that weaken the tree. Extra-long, heavy, horizontal limbs put a great strain on any tree and will probably eventually split off, so you should remove them early on. Also, take out limbs at acute angles to the trunk, particularly ones that form crotches at 45 degrees or less. Although home growers don't usually prune to increase nut yields, commercial orchardists boost production by cutting out old wood and thinning out the branches to allow in more light.

If you need to cut off heavy limbs for any reason, do it in stages, as shown on pages 62–63. Never seal cuts or cavities with tree dressing or paint. If you remove the branch properly at the branch collar, the tree itself will seal the wound.

Almonds

Q I planted a pair of almond trees a year ago. How should I prune them?

A The almond (*Prunus dulcis*) is a member of the rose family, as are the plum, peach, and other stone-fruit trees, and it closely resembles them in its growth habit. Different varieties grow in different shapes — some are low and bushy and others are more upright. Your pruning should conform to your tree's natural growth habit. If you care for it properly, your almond will produce for 50 years or more.

Almonds are usually pruned during dormancy, though some California almond growers achieve good results pruning in fall. Train the young tree into an open or modified leader form (see How to Shape Fruit Trees, pages 224–225). Avoid unnecessary pruning, as that will stimulate extra leaf growth and delay bearing.

Q Do mature almond trees need much pruning?

A Almonds bear nuts on short, stubby spurs. These trees need little pruning, and yields may decrease if you prune too much. Prune to let sunlight penetrate the branches, just as you would a fruit tree.

Chestnuts

Q Can I grow American chestnuts, or were they all destroyed by blight?

A American chestnut (*Castanea dentata*) has a naturally spreading vase-shaped habit. Sadly, most of these trees succumbed to the chestnut blight that swept the country in the early 1900s. The few trees that survived have been propagated and crossed with imported, blight-resistant types, so there are now several varieties of chestnut available. None is entirely blight-proof, but some are quite resistant.

Q I like chestnut trees, but the American hybrids are too big for my lot. Can pruning keep them small?

A If you don't have enough space or simply prefer a smaller tree, consider the widely planted Chinese chestnut (*Castanea mollissima*), which grows 35 to 40 feet high. Chinese chestnut resists blight and produces nuts that are tasty but less sweet than the American species. As with most nut trees, you need to plant two cultivars for pollination.

Q I just planted a pair of Chinese chestnuts. What's the best way to prune them?

A For both Chinese and hybrid chestnuts, guide the tree to a modified central leader (see How to Shape Fruit Trees, pages 224–225) with a balanced branch formation. Keep the trunk clear of branches up to a height of 8 feet, never removing more than 25 percent of the crown at one time, preferably less. As the tree matures, the shape of the crown may be hard to maintain as aging branches spread and droop. Bearing trees need little pruning.

Q When should I prune my chestnut trees?

A Chestnuts don't need annual pruning, but if yours need some work, it's best to prune when the trees are dormant, not in spring or summer.

Filberts

 I have a small garden. Are there any nuts I can grow?

Filberts and hazelnuts (*Corylus* spp.) stay small, so they suit the home garden better than most nut trees. They range from the small native American hazelnut (*C. avelana*) to improved and named varieties of the European filbert, the only member of the species cultivated to any extent. Choose either a self-pollinated filbert like 'Winkler' or plant two cultivars to assure cross-pollination. Unlike many nut trees, the filbert lacks a deep-growing taproot, so it is much easier to transplant.

You can start new plants from seeds or via layers. To layer, bend over a low branch and cover the middle section with soil so that it can root. Because filberts are easily propagated in this way, they are seldom grafted.

 When should I prune my filbert?

 Prune when dormant, from late fall to early spring.

Q I bought a grafted filbert. Should it be pruned differently from filberts grown on their own roots?

A If you have a grafted tree, be especially careful to prune away all the suckers growing around the bottom of the main stem so they won't crowd out the good part of the tree. Prune most of the suckers growing from the roots of a non-grafted tree also, to keep the tree from getting too bushy.

Q Do mature filberts require pruning?

A Mature filberts need pruning mostly to keep them in shape and to let more light into the tree. Cut out some old branches when dormant, and new ones will replace them.

Q How do I prune my filbert?

A Filberts are usually grown as shrubs or large bushes, except in the West, where they are pruned into a tree form with a single main stem. If you are growing your filbert as a bush, keep it pruned to five or six main stems so it won't become too wide and unmanageable.

Pecans and Hickories

Q My neighbor says I can dig a couple of hickory seedlings from the back of his property. Are they easy to transplant?

A The hickory family is native to the central part of North America and includes the shagbark (*Carya ovata*), mockernut (*C. tomentosa*), pignut (*C. glabra*), and shellbark (*C. laciniosa*), as well as pecan (*C. illinoinensis*). Some hickories are ornamental and some (pecan, shagbark, and shellbark) produce high-quality nuts.

To anchor a tree this size, nature equips hickory with a long taproot that develops early in life. Thus, planting or moving even a small tree is not easy. When starting a new tree, unless you want to try one of the hybrids, plant it where you want it to grow so you won't have to move it later. Never prune the taproot, and take special care to keep it safe during planting.

Q When's the best time to prune a hickory?

A Prune when the tree is dormant so you can see its form and to lessen chances of disease transmission.

Q Can you give me some guidelines for pruning hickories?

A Train to a central leader, and remove crossed branches. Remove the lower limbs as the young trees grow, so that by the time they are 15 feet tall, none will be closer than 6 to 8 feet from the ground. If growing your trees for lumber, prune higher as a tree continues to grow.

Pruning mature hickories is not usually necessary or practical because of their great height (up to 100 feet). They tend to grow upright, and have a naturally strong central leader.

SEE ALSO: *Training Shade Trees*, page 80.

Q What do I need to know to grow pecans?

A Pecan (*Carya illinoinensis*), one of the best-known edible hickories, is native to the central and southeastern United States, but you can find suitable cultivars for most parts of the country. Although primarily a commercial nut, it also grows extensively on farms and in backyard gardens. Some newer pecan varieties are smaller and less upright their native relatives, making them more suitable for the home garden. A few are self-fertile, and thus don't need a second tree for pollination.

Pecans have long, deep taproots, and they need the same care you'd give any of the hickories when you're planting the small trees. Never cut or bend the taproot during the moving process. Plant at least two, preferably three, cultivars for maximum yield.

Q How do I prune the young pecan tree I just planted?

A Train in its early years so it will grow with a strong central leader. Make sure branches are well spaced with strong connections to the trunk and no bark wedged between them. Because of pest, disease, and structural issues, these are high-maintenance trees that may need some professional care. Although you can do light pruning when needed, do major pruning, such as the removal of lower or damaged limbs, only when the tree is dormant.

Prune away a few bottom limbs each year, until it has 6 to 8 feet of branch-free lower trunk. If you grow a disease-resistant cultivar, this may be the only pruning a backyard tree will ever need.

Walnuts and Butternuts

Q Is there much difference between butternut and black walnut trees?

A These North American members of the walnut family are valued for their nuts and their lumber. They look so much alike when they're young that it's difficult to tell them apart, but their nuts look very different. Although the butternut (*Juglans cinerea*) is hardier than the black walnut (*J. nigra*), both grow well throughout most of the eastern United States and southern Canada.

Both butternut and black walnut trees have very strong wood, so they need less pruning than most trees. The unusual crotches that insist on growing may be less hazardous to the trees' health than they would be on weaker trees.

Q Which method should I use to train my new black walnut tree?

A Train it to grow with a strong central leader for its first few years. The terminal bud is easily damaged by weather, and if this happens, two or three sprouts will grow. Don't let the tree grow into a bush — keep pinching and snipping it into one main trunk for as long as possible.

Don't wait until the tree is fully grown to start cutting off the bottom limbs. Large wounds don't close well, and the trunk will permanently show a scar.

If you are growing the tree for its nuts, site it 30 to 40 feet from other trees. If you are growing your tree for lumber, it's especially important to grow it with a strong central leader, so that you'll have logs that are straight and free of large limbs.

SEE ALSO: *Training Shade Trees, page 80.*

Q How should I prune mature butternuts and black walnuts?

A As the trees grow taller, prune off a few of the lower branches each year. Spread major pruning over several years, always leaving at least twice as much branched area as you have limb-free trunk. Never reduce the leaf space by more than 25 percent in any year.

Q I eat lots of walnuts and want to grow some trees in my yard. Which type should I grow?

A Although black walnut trees are native to eastern North America, English walnuts are the commercial walnut that you buy at the store. Persian walnut (*Juglans regia*) is the true name of the common or English walnut, which arrived in the colonies on English ships. Actually, the cool climate of the British Isles is not at all suitable for the culture of the Persian walnut, because it needs continuous warmth to grow well.

Since the introduction of the Carpathian strain of Persian walnut from Poland (*Juglans regia* var. *carpathian*), these trees grow in home gardens all over the country and are no longer restricted to the more temperate West Coast. Careful breeding and seed selection are slowly extending the growing region into the northern states and southern Canada. If you're buying new walnut trees, ask about the growth and bearing habits of your cultivar so you'll know how to prune them.

Most walnuts in commercial groves — and even some of those growing in backyard gardens — are grafted, often onto black walnut seedlings. It's easy to see a difference in the bark below and above the graft on these trees. To grow just one tree, buy a self-fruitful cultivar such as 'Colby' or 'Hansen'.

DISEASE ALERT

The survival of butternut in North America is at risk from butternut canker, *Sirococcus clavigignenti-juglandacearum,* a fungal disease spread during the growing season by wind and splashing rain. Another butternut fungus, *Melanconis juglandis,* produces secondary infections that cause branch dieback but not cankers. To minimize risk of disease, prune butternut minimally and only when dormant. Make sure the tree surface is dry before cutting, and sterilize pruning tools before and after each cut.

Q My English walnut needs some pruning. When is the best time?

A Walnuts bleed heavily when pruned in late winter to early spring. That bleeding will not hurt the tree, but if you find it unsightly, prune in late fall after leaf drop or wait until summer.

Q Does my new English walnut need any special care?

A The bark of young walnut trees sunscalds so easily that you should whitewash the trunk of a newly planted tree or cover it with tree wrap for the first few years.

Q How do I prune a young English walnut?

A Remove suckers growing from the base (below the graft); they're not the nut you want, plus they look unattractive and sap energy from the tree. Some walnut hybrids bear such heavy crops of nuts that you should prune them to grow with a modified central

leader to encourage wide, sturdy crotches. It's also important to remove all branches to about 8 feet above the ground as soon as the tree is tall enough to permit this safely. Prune off competing suckers.

Q How do I prune a mature English walnut?

A A mature walnut needs occasional pruning to let more light into the interior of the tree. Cut out some old, unproductive wood and let new, young branches replace it. Prune off sagging branches hindering the tree's development.

In later years, some varieties — 'Mayette', for instance — tend to be of such spreading growth that an open-center method of pruning is best (see How to Shape Fruit Trees, pages 224–225). Commercial growers who plant walnuts in large orchards prune them so that they can harvest the nuts with a mechanical shaker. Most homeowners shake the tree themselves, so tree shape isn't as important.

Plant-by-Plant Pruning Guide

FOR ORNAMENTAL TREES, SHRUBS, AND VINES

This section provides garden-ready pruning information on more than 160 trees, shrubs, ground covers, and woody herbs and vines, including the plants mentioned in the main text. When reading this guide, keep the following points in mind:

- When and what to prune depends upon your pruning goal. Don't prune without a reason.
- Remove dead, damaged, and diseased branches at any time.
- Remove crossed and rubbing branches.
- As long as you remove less than 15 percent of the leaves, prune when needed and at your convenience.
- Do heavy pruning of most plants before buds break in late winter or early spring. This will reduce flowering that year for trees and shrubs blooming on old wood. It does not affect plants blooming on new growth.
- Don't prune plants when they're wet.
- Don't prune in late summer and early fall, as new growth may not have time to harden off before winter.
- To minimize pruning, pick a species or variety that will grow to the size you want.

KEY TO PRUNING METHODS

For instructions and illustrations on each pruning method, see the page listed below.

- **Candling** (pinching off soft new growth on some types of evergreens), pages 137–138
- **Cleanup** (removing dead, diseased, damaged growth), page 11
- **Coppicing** (cutting trees and shrubs almost to the ground), page 190
- **Deadheading** (removing faded flowers), page 99
- **Espalier** (training into a two-dimensional pattern on a wall, trellis, or wires), pages 180–184
- **Head back** (prune to an outward-facing bud or branch within canopy), page 52, 61
- **Limbing up** (removing lower branches), page 64
- **Pinching** (squeezing off soft new shoots between thumbnail and forefinger), page 57
- **Pollarding** (similar to coppicing, but higher off the ground), page 193
- **Pruning as standard** (shaping into a round leafy crown above a short, single trunk), page 179
- **Renewal** (rejuvenating old plants by removing one-quarter to one-third of the oldest wood each year until all old wood is gone), page 101
- **Renovating** (cutting back stems to 6 to 12 inches above the ground), page 190
- **Root pruning** (trimming the roots, often used for potted plants), page 70

- **Shaping** (controlling direction of growth and overall size), pages 16–20
- **Shearing** (removing the ends of shoots for a smooth overall shape; it causes dense, twiggy growth below the cuts), page 59
- **Shrub-to-tree** (turning a shrub into a small tree with a single trunk), pages 104–105
- **Sucker removal** (pruning unwanted shoots from the rootstock and water sprouts from branches), page 98
- **Thinning** (cutting stems and branches back to a trunk, big side branch, or the ground), page 63
- **Topiary** (cutting to a decorative shape), page 175
- **Training** (directing the structural growth of a young plant by selective branch removal), see the appropriate chapter for the type of plant.

BOTANICAL NAME	COMMON NAME	HABIT	SHAPE	PRUNING METHODS	
Abelia grandiflora	GLOSSY ABELIA	Semi-evergreen to deciduous shrub	Rounded	Thinning, renovating	
Abies spp.	FIR	Needled evergreen trees	Pyramidal	Cleanup	
Acer griseum	PAPERBARK MAPLE	Deciduous tree	Vase	Limbing up	
Acer palmatum	JAPANESE MAPLE	Deciduous single- or multi-stemmed tree or shrub	Rounded or weeping (depends on cultivar)	Thinning	
Acer rubrum	RED MAPLE	Deciduous tree	Rounded	Training, cleanup	
Actinidia spp.	KIWI, SIBERIAN GOOSE-BERRY, KOLOMIKTA VINE	Deciduous twining vines	Vine	Shaping	
Aesculus glabra	OHIO BUCKEYE	Deciduous tree	Rounded	Training, cleanup, limbing up	

TIME	PRUNING TIPS
Late winter to early spring	Flowers on new wood. Remove dead stems in early spring; cut back overgrown or unbalanced specimens to ground.
Late winter to early spring, or as needed	Needs little pruning except for a dead or broken branch. Limbing up wrecks the shape, so plant where that won't be necessary.
Late winter to early spring	Enjoy the rich peeling coppery bark by removing lower limbs. Sap flow after dormant pruning will not hurt the tree; can prune in midsummer for less flowing sap.
Late winter to early spring	Architecture usually pleasing, needs little if any improvement. If needed, thin some twiggy interior growth in cut-leaf specimens. Sap flow after dormant pruning will not hurt the tree; can prune in midsummer for less flowing sap.
Late winter to early spring for major work	Treat red maple, sugar maple (*A. saccharum*), and Norway maple (*A. platanoides*) as shade trees; train for strong structure as described in chapter 5. Sap flow from dormant pruning will not hurt tree.
Late winter to early spring, cut stray shoots as needed	Do major pruning when dormant but leave some old wood since plants bloom on wood at least a year old. For fruit production, leave 8 to 10 buds. To curb growth, cut back wild shoots in early to midsummer.
Late winter to early spring	Prune off lower limbs as trees grow. Remove unsightly or dangerous limbs on older trees.

BOTANICAL NAME	COMMON NAME	HABIT	SHAPE	PRUNING METHODS	
Akebia quinata	FIVE-LEAF AKEBIA, CHOCOLATE VINE	Deciduous twining vine	Vine	Shaping, renovating	
Alnus glutinosa	BLACK ALDER	Deciduous tree	Pyramidal to rounded	Training	
Amelanchier spp.	SHADBUSH, SERVICE-BERRY	Deciduous trees or shrubs	Oval to rounded	Cleanup, training	
Aralia elata	JAPANESE ANGELICA	Deciduous shrub or small tree	Rounded to spreading	Sucker removal, shrub-to-tree	
Arbutus menziesii	MADRONE	Broadleaf evergreen tree	Rounded to irregular	Limb-ing up, cleanup	
Arctostaphylos uva-ursi	BEARBERRY	Evergreen ground cover	Mat	Cleanup, shaping	
Aristolochia durior	DUTCH-MAN'S-PIPE	Deciduous twining vine	Vine	Cleanup	
Aucuba japonica	GOLD DUST PLANT	Broadleaf evergreen shrub	Rounded	Thinning, renovating	

TIME	PRUNING TIPS
Varies with goal	Blooms on old wood. Rank grower; prune hard in late spring after flowers fade. Summer pruning will reduce flowering. Every 10 or 12 years, cut to ground in early spring.
Late winter to early spring	Prune for central leader, strong framework. Respect the tree's naturally layered shape.
Late winter to early spring	Needs little pruning. Prune only to shape, as either a bush or a tree.
Late winter to early spring	Remove suckers right away. Green-leaved suckers on variegated cultivars can overwhelm the desirable plant growing above the rootstock.
Late winter to early spring	Remove diseased limbs and stray branches. Remove lower limbs to show off colorful bark.
As needed	Prune as necessary to remove dead or damaged parts. Well behaved; requires little to no pruning, except to control spread.
Late winter to early spring	Little to no pruning except to keep under control and to remove wayward dangling stems. Cut off old wood and winter injury.
Late winter to early spring	Rarely needs pruning. Thin to control size and give the air circulation it requires for good health. Renovate if stems grow too long or look bare at base.

BOTANICAL NAME	COMMON NAME	HABIT	SHAPE	PRUNING METHODS	
Berberis spp.	BARBERRY	Deciduous and evergreen shrubs	Rounded	Renovating, shearing, cleanup	
Betula spp.	BIRCH	Deciduous multistem or single-trunk trees	Pyramidal, rounded, or weeping	Limbing up, cleanup	
Bignonia capreolata	CROSS VINE	Evergreen to semi-evergreen clinging vine	Vine	Shaping	
Buddleia alternifolia	ALTERNATE-LEAF BUTTERFLY BUSH	Deciduous shrub	Rounded, weeping	Thinning, pruning as standard	
Buddleia davidii	BUTTERFLY BUSH	Deciduous shrub	Rounded	Coppicing, thinning, deadheading	
Buxus spp.	BOXWOOD	Evergreen shrubs or small trees	Rounded	Shearing, topiary	

TIME	PRUNING TIPS
Depends on goal	Remove weak crossing branches; head back to encourage denser growth. Clip lightly in summer, or frequently and severely for a formal look. When bushes begin to deteriorate, renovate in late winter or early spring.
Late winter to early spring	Limb up river (*B. nigra*), paper (*B. papyrifera*), European white (*B. pendula*), gray (*B. populifolia*), and white-barked Himalayan birches (*B. utilis* var. *jacquemontii*) to show off their attractive bark. Like maples, birches bleed when pruned during dormancy, but sap does no harm.
Late winter to early spring	Grows up to 20 ft. a year; control by pruning and shaping when dormant. Remove weak or wayward stems; mow or dig out excess root shoots.
After bloom	Blooms on old wood; prune after flowers fade in early summer. Cut to ground one-quarter to one-third of oldest stems and cut back remaining stems by one-third. Or grow as a standard by pruning to one stem; cut back stems by half after bloom.
Late winter to early spring	Blooms on new wood. Dies to the ground in cold winters; cut back to 6 to 12 in. before new growth begins. In warmer climates grows up to 12 ft. tall and gets unruly; clip stray stems or renovate each year when dormant.
Shear in summer; do heavy pruning in late spring	Shears beautifully. Shear several times a season to get a tight formal effect or clip selected branches for a naturalistic look. In heavy snow country, keep top rounded or pointed to prevent crushing by snow.

BOTANICAL NAME	COMMON NAME	HABIT	SHAPE	PRUNING METHODS	
Callicarpa spp.	PURPLE BEAUTY-BERRY	Deciduous shrubs	Rounded	Renovating	
Calluna vulgaris	SCOTCH HEATHER	Shrubby ground cover	Spreading	Shearing, deadhead-ing	
Calocedrus decurrens	CALIFORNIA INCENSE CEDAR	Evergreen tree	Columnar	Thinning, shearing	
Camellia spp.	CAMELLIA	Broadleaf evergreen shrubs or small trees	Pyramidal	Thinning, cleanup, espalier	
Campsis radicans	TRUMPET CREEPER	Deciduous twining and cling-ing vine	Vine	Shaping, renewal	
Carpinus spp.	HORNBEAM	Deciduous trees	Rounded	Training, thinning, shearing, topiary	
Carya spp.	HICKORY	Deciduous trees	Oval	Training, shearing, cleanup	

TIME	PRUNING TIPS
Late winter to early spring	Blooms on new wood. Cut back to 1 ft. every few years to keep bushy. In colder areas, cut back each spring if plant's top is killed back in winter.
Early spring in cold climates, late fall to early winter in warm ones; after bloom for winter bloomers	Each year, remove dead flowers or cut back flowering stems when dormant (after flowers fade in Zone 6 and warmer). Cut only green stems, not woody ones.
Late winter to early spring	Has a naturally strong form, needs little pruning. Can shear to control size or make foliage appear thicker.
After bloom, before new growth starts	Seldom needs pruning. Removing weak branches and some interior twigs improves air circulation. For bigger blooms, disbud before flowers open.
Late winter to early spring	Prune to keep from becoming too heavy. Cut off flowers as they fade; cut dangling and trailing branches. Remove suckers.
Late winter to early spring	Shade trees need little pruning except to maintain a strong single trunk and rounded canopy. European hornbeam (*C. betulus*) tolerates severe pruning for slow-growing, dense formal hedges or topiary.
Late winter to early spring	Train for strong structure when young; take out competing leaders and weak branches to enhance natural shape. Prune off dead, diseased branches and witches'-brooms.

BOTANICAL NAME	COMMON NAME	HABIT	SHAPE	PRUNING METHODS	
Caryopteris × clandonensis	BLUEBEARD	Deciduous shrub	Rounded	Renovating	
Catalpa bignonioides	SOUTHERN CATALPA, INDIAN BEAN TREE	Deciduous tree	Rounded to spreading	Training, thinning, limbing up	
Cedrus spp.	CEDAR	Needled evergreen trees	Pyramidal	Cleanup	
Celastrus scandens	AMERICAN BITTER-SWEET	Deciduous twining vine	Vine	Shaping, sucker removal, renovating	
Celtis occidentalis	HACKBERRY	Deciduous tree	Vase to spreading and irregular	Training, limbing up	
Cephalanthus occidentalis	BUTTON-BUSH	Deciduous shrub	Rounded	Thinning, renewal, renovating, shrub-to-tree	
Cephalotaxus harringtonii	JAPANESE PLUM YEW	Needled evergreen shrub	Rounded, spreading	Thinning, cleanup, renewal, renovating	
Cercidi-phyllum japonicum	KATSURA	Deciduous tree	Rounded (pyramidal when young)	Training, thinning, limbing up	

TIME	PRUNING TIPS
Late winter to early spring	Blooms on new growth. Cut back hard in late winter or early spring.
Late winter to early spring	Brittle wood may break in ice storms; prune for strong structure. Thin canopy by removing competing leaders, limbs that rub, and crossed or weak branches with narrow crotches.
Late winter to early spring	Little pruning needed if given space to expand. Thin out dead wood.
Late winter to early spring	Remove suckers any time. Clip off fruiting wood annually. Prune unkempt old vines back to 1 ft. to renovate. Don't confuse this native with invasive Oriental bittersweet (*C. orbiculatus*), which fruits on side shoots instead of at tips.
Late winter to early spring	Prune when young for single trunk with strong branch attachments. Forming a strong scaffold may take several years. Limb up to showcase striking warty bark.
Early spring	Renovate unkempt shrubs by cutting to ground. Or, renew over three to four years. Limb up some strong attractive stems for multi-trunk tree.
Late winter to early spring, or as needed	Needs little pruning. Like yew, can sprout on old bare wood and tolerates severe pruning. Cut back leggy shrubs to 6 to 12 in. high. Thin dead wood when needed.
Late winter to early spring	Needs little pruning if trained to single trunk with strong scaffold branches. For trees with multiple trunks, thin and limb up to reduce weight on branches.

BOTANICAL NAME	COMMON NAME	HABIT	SHAPE	PRUNING METHODS	
Cercis spp.	REDBUD	Deciduous small trees	Rounded to irregular (vase when young)	Training, cleanup	
Chaenomeles spp.	FLOWERING QUINCE	Deciduous shrubs	Rounded, irregular	Thinning, cleanup, sucker removal, renewal, renovating	
Chamaecyparis spp.	FALSE CYPRESS	Evergreen trees or shrubs	Pyramid	Shearing, cleanup, thinning	
Chionanthus spp.	FRINGE TREE, OLD-MAN'S BEARD	Deciduous trees	Rounded	Cleanup, shrub-to-tree	
Clematis spp.	CLEMATIS	Deciduous twining vines; a few are deciduous shrubs	Vine	Shaping	
Clethra spp.	CLETHRA, SUMMER-SWEET, JAPANESE CLETHRA	Deciduous shrubs	Oval to spreading or rounded (depends on species)	Thinning, sucker removal, renewal, shrub-to-tree	

TIME	PRUNING TIPS
After bloom	Blooms on old wood. Train to single or multiple trunks. Needs occasional removal of dead or diseased branches.
After bloom	Thin out a few old leggy stems each year and any crossed, rubbing, dead, and diseased branches. Shorten twiggy, drooping branches that touch the ground. Clip suckers. Renovate by cutting near ground.
Late winter to early spring, small stuff any time	Use clippers to remove overly long stems; leave no stubs. Can shear, but cut only green growth and never into old bare wood.
After bloom	Needs minimal pruning. Train as a single or multi-trunk tree.
Depends on growing group; see clematis in chapter 10	Shrubby species such as *C. heracleifolia* and *C. integrifolia* flower best on new growth and can be pruned hard in early spring.
Late winter to early spring	Cut out a few oldest stems each year; remove suckers to control spread. To display peeling bark of Japanese clethra (*C. berbinervis*), remove lower limbs. Ground covers such as *C. alnifolia* 'Hummingbird' may need renovating.

BOTANICAL NAME	COMMON NAME	HABIT	SHAPE	PRUNING METHODS	
Cornus spp.	DOGWOOD	Deciduous shrubs or small single- or multi-trunk trees	Rounded	Training, cleanup, coppicing (shrubs)	
Cotinus spp.	SMOKE-BUSH, AMERICAN SMOKETREE	Deciduous shrubs or small trees	Rounded	Cleanup, thinning, renewal, pollarding, coppicing	
Cotoneaster spp.	COTON-EASTER	Deciduous, semi-ever-green, or evergreen ground covers or shrubs	Spreading or rounded (depends on species)	Shaping, cleanup, renewal, shearing, espalier	
Crataegus spp.	HAWTHORN	Deciduous trees	Oval, vase, or rounded	Training, cleanup, shrub renewal, shearing	
Cryptomeria japonica	JAPANESE CEDAR	Evergreen tree	Pyramidal	Cleanup	

TIME	PRUNING TIPS
Late winter to early spring (major pruning)	Don't prune in May, June, and July, when borers are active. Prune flowering dogwood (*C. florida*) as little as possible because cuts heal slowly. Kousa dogwood (*C. kousa*) usually needs no pruning unless limbed up to show off flaking bark. Train cornelian cherry (*C. mas*) as a big shrub, erect tree, or deciduous hedge. Prune *C. alternifolia* and *C. controversa* to maintain layered growth habit. Coppice redtwig dogwoods (*C. alba* and *C. sericea*) every year or two for colorful bark.
Late winter to early spring	Renew by removing a few branches at a time over several years. Blooms on two-year growth; pruning keeps them denser and more compact but reduces flowering. Or once plants are a couple of years old, coppice for extra-big leaves and no flowers (pollard for taller plants).
Late winter to early spring	Cut back ground covers (*C. apiculatus, C. horizontalis,* and *C. nanshan*) hard to renovate. Cut back stray shoots on *C. dammeri* and *C. salicifolius* 'Repens' after bloom. Instead of shearing *C. divaricatus*, prune selected branches to the base. Can shear hedge cotoneaster (*C. lucidus*).
Late winter or after bloom	Train to a single trunk and prune out narrow crotches. In summer clip lightly for informal barrier or shear for dense, formal appearance. Prune fire blight–infected wood about 1 ft. below blackened leaves and discolored wood; sterilize tools between cuts; bag or burn prunings.
Late winter to early spring	Remove winter damage on tree in exposed location. Can cut back overgrown tree to 3 ft. and it will resprout.

BOTANICAL NAME	COMMON NAME	HABIT	SHAPE	PRUNING METHODS	
Cunninghamia lanceolata	CHINA FIR	Needled evergreen tree	Pyramidal (opens up with age)	Cleanup	
Cupressus macrocarpa	MONTEREY CYPRESS	Evergreen tree	Pyramidal (spreads and flattens with age)	Cleanup	
Cytisus spp.	BROOM	Deciduous shrubs	Rounded to spreading	Renovating	
Daphne spp.	DAPHNE	Deciduous, semi-evergreen, or evergreen shrubs	Rounded to spreading	Cleanup, renewal	
Deutzia spp.	DEUTZIA	Deciduous shrubs	Rounded	Renewal, sucker removal	
Diervilla sessilifolia	SOUTHERN BUSH HONEY-SUCKLE	Deciduous shrub	Rounded, suckering	Cleanup, sucker removal	
Distictis buccinatoria	BLOOD TRUMPET	Evergreen clinging vine	Vine	Shaping	

TIME	PRUNING TIPS
Late winter to early spring	Remove winter-killed or damaged branches but do not overprune.
Early to midsummer	Little pruning beyond thinning out dead wood; constant removal of foliage isn't good for it. Hard pruning in winter damages nutrient supply to roots and may kill tree. Cut back and burn canker-infected limbs; remove the whole tree if infection is severe.
After bloom	Prune new green growth back by half to two-thirds annually right after flowering to keep bushy and prevent setting seed. (Invasive in much of North America.)
After bloom	Doesn't need much pruning. Clean out dead wood and snip stray shoots after flowering. Renew old bushes over three years.
After bloom	For bushy growth, cut back flowering stems by one-third when blossoms start to fade; thin to the ground one-third of oldest stems. To control spread, prune off suckers or dig up and replant elsewhere.
Late winter to early spring	Flowers on new wood. When grown informally, needs little pruning. To restrict spread, dig out suckers.
Late winter to early spring	Prune as you would ivy (*Hedera* spp.).

BOTANICAL NAME	COMMON NAME	HABIT	SHAPE	PRUNING METHODS	
Erica carnea	SPRING HEATH	Evergreen shrub, ground cover	Spreading	Cleanup, shearing	
Euonymus alatus	BURNING BUSH	Deciduous shrub	Rounded	Cleanup, thinning, shrub-to-tree, shearing, renovating	
Euonymus fortunei	WINTER CREEPER	Evergreen cling-ing vine, ground cover, or shrub	Vine, mat, or spreading	Shaping, cleanup, espalier, shearing	
Fagus spp.	EUROPEAN BEECH	Deciduous trees	Spreading (oval when young)	Training, limb-ing up, thinning	
Fallopia baldschuanica	SILVER LACE VINE	Deciduous twining vine	Vine	Shaping	
Fatsia japonica	JAPANESE FATSIA	Evergreen shrub or multi-trunk tree	Rounded	Sucker removal, coppicing, renovating, shrub-to-tree	

TIME	PRUNING TIPS
After bloom	Needs little pruning; remove dead wood and winter injury. Cut into green stems only, not lower woody parts. Clip tops lightly, and tidy edges of the clump.
Late winter to early spring	Shapely in full sun; in shade the plant opens up to an irregular form. Takes well to hard pruning; shear to keep small. Limb up to turn shrub into a small, multistemmed tree. Invasive in many areas.
Late winter to early spring; light pruning at any time	Prune hard to keep within bounds.
Late winter to early spring	Train to a central leader with strong framework because of heavy limbs with crotchy tendencies. Wait several years to limb up to avoid sunscald of attractive bark. Also handsome with low, wide-spreading branches left on the tree.
Late winter to early spring	Fast growing; needs annual shaping to keep in check. Remove wayward growth and weak, dead, diseased, or damaged stems.
Late winter to early spring	Requires little pruning but tolerates hard pruning. To keep small, dig out suckers and remove overly long stems. Limb up for a 12-ft. multi-trunk tree.

BOTANICAL NAME	COMMON NAME	HABIT	SHAPE	PRUNING METHODS	
Forsythia × intermedia	FORSYTHIA	Deciduous shrub	Rounded, suckering	Sucker removal, thinning, coppicing, shearing, renovating	
Fothergilla spp.	FOTHER-GILLA	Deciduous shrubs	Rounded, suckering	Thinning, sucker removal	
Franklinia alatamaha	FRANKLIN TREE	Deciduous multi-trunk tree	Rounded	Thinning, shrub-to-tree, cleanup	
Fraxinus spp.	ASH	Deciduous trees	Pyramidal, rounded, or irregular (depends on species, cultivar)	Thinning, training, limbing up	
Gardenia jasminoides	GARDENIA	Evergreen shrub	Rounded	Pinching, thinning, renovating, deadheading	
Garrya elliptica	SILK-TASSEL	Broadleaf evergreen shrub or small tree	Vase	Cleanup, renewal	

TIME	PRUNING TIPS
After bloom	Thin some old growth each year right after flowering. Renovate unkempt shrubs in late winter, sacrificing that season's blooms. Tight, formal hedges need more than one shearing, which removes next year's flower buds.
After bloom	Needs little pruning. To control growth, remove some suckers and thin out tallest stems at the base. Leave some suckers to prevent a leggy look.
Late winter to early spring	Doesn't need much pruning; just remove dead or diseased branches. Can train to one trunk.
Late winter to early spring	Prune to correct multiple weak trunks and poorly attached branches. Train to central leader with strong limbs well spaced around the tree.
After bloom	Needs only a little thinning to maintain rounded form. Pinch back young shrubs to increase bushiness. If winterkilled or overgrown, cut to 6 to 12 in. For maximum bloom, do not prune after September in warm climates.
As tassels fade but before new growth begins	Provide enough room to grow without pruning. If overgrown, renew over three or four years.

BOTANICAL NAME	COMMON NAME	HABIT	SHAPE	PRUNING METHODS	
Ginkgo biloba	GINKGO	Deciduous tree	Spreading and irregular (pyramidal when young)	Limbing up	
Gleditsia triacanthos var. *inermis*	THORNLESS HONEY LOCUST	Deciduous tree	Rounded	Training, limbing up, shearing	
Halesia carolina	CAROLINA SILVERBELL	Single or multi-trunk deciduous flowering tree	Rounded	Training	
Hammamelis × intermedia	HYBRID WITCH HAZEL	Deciduous shrub	Rounded or vase to spreading	Sucker removal, thinning	
Hedera spp.	IVY	Evergreen clinging vines or ground covers	Vine	Shaping	
Heptacodium miconioides	SEVEN-SON FLOWER	Shrub or small tree	Irregular	Thinning, shrub-to-tree	

TIME	PRUNING TIPS
Late winter to early spring	Emphasize height by removing lower limbs; otherwise prune as little as possible. Females have stinky fall fruits; plant male cultivar.
Late winter to early spring	Train to a central leader when young and for as long as possible. For barrier hedge, plant thorny species and shear heavily. Clip lightly in summer for informal barrier or prune frequently and severely for more formal look.
After bloom	Rarely needs pruning. Typically multi-trunk, but can train to a single trunk when young.
After bloom	Little pruning needed. Dig out suckers to restrict expansion. Prune to bud or branch inside crown to lower height. Prune fall-flowering native species (*H. virginiana*) when dormant.
Any time	Prune ruthlessly any time. Cut off torn, dangling pieces and stems over doors and windows. Remove parts growing too high.
Late winter to early spring	Thin back awkward shoots to a larger branch; otherwise let it be. If you're into its gorgeous peeling bark, limb up into a small single or multi-trunk tree.

BOTANICAL NAME	COMMON NAME	HABIT	SHAPE	PRUNING METHODS	
Hibiscus syriacus	ROSE OF SHARON	Deciduous shrub	Oval	Cleanup, shrub-to-tree, shearing, renovating, espalier	
Hydrangea anomala subsp. *petiolaris*	CLIMBING HYDRANGEA	Deciduous clinging vine or ground cover	Vine or mat	Cleanup, shaping	
Hydrangea arborescens	SMOOTH HYDRANGEA	Deciduous shrub	Rounded	Cleanup, renovating	
Hydrangea macrophylla	BIG-LEAF HYDRANGEA	Deciduous shrub	Rounded	Deadheading, renovating, cleanup	
Hydrangea paniculata 'Grandiflora'	PEEGEE HYDRANGEA	Deciduous shrub or small tree	Rounded to spreading	Cleanup, sucker removal, shrub-to-tree, renewal, renovating	

TIME	PRUNING TIPS
Spring	Leafs out late. Thin dead, damaged wood. Blooms on new wood, so renovated shrub will bloom the following season. Turn into small tree by selecting one or more strong stems and eliminating the rest. To eliminate seedlings, shear after bloom but before seeds set. Evergreen hibiscus (*H. rosa-sinensis*) needs tips pinched in early summer for a bushy plant.
Early spring	Blooms on old wood. If needed, prune in early spring to control growth and remove loose, hanging, or dead parts. Prune stray shoots as they appear in summer.
Late winter to early spring	Blooms on new wood. Cut back hard before new growth begins for bigger blooms and neater form.
After bloom	Little pruning needed. Blooms on tips of year-old wood, so prune when flowers are fading. If winter kills top, cut to ground, sacrificing one year's bloom. For minor winterkill, tip pruning in early spring may force flower buds lower down on the branches to grow.
Late winter to early spring	Remove weak, crossing, and rubbing branches and some oldest, tallest branches. To control size or renovate, cut nearly to ground (or, for a bigger bush, to a live outward bud). For bigger flower clusters, thin to 5 to 10 shoots.

BOTANICAL NAME	COMMON NAME	HABIT	SHAPE	PRUNING METHODS	
Hydrangea quercifolia	OAKLEAF HYDRANGEA	Deciduous shrub	Rounded to spreading	Renewal, cleanup	
Hypericum calycinum	SAINT-JOHN'S-WORT, AARON'S BEARD	Evergreen to semi-evergreen ground cover	Spreading	Reno-vating, shearing, shaping	
Ilex crenata	JAPANESE HOLLY	Broadleaf evergreen shrub	Rounded	Thinning, shearing, topiary	
Ilex × meserveae	BLUE HOLLY	Broadleaf evergreen shrub or small tree	Pyrami-dal or rounded	Thinning, shearing	
Ilex verticillata	WINTER-BERRY	Deciduous shrub	Spreading, suckering	Renewal, sucker removal	

TIME	PRUNING TIPS
After bloom	Prune before the next year's buds are set. Remove dead wood. Thin to renew or reduce size, removing one-third of oldest stems for three years. Stop pruning by the end of July or you may affect next year's flowering.
Late winter to early spring	Blooms on new wood. In cold climates may die back to ground, resprouting from base each spring. To keep bushy in warm climates, shear or cut to the ground every few years.
Early summer to midsummer	Rarely needs pruning, but tolerates shearing and heavy pruning. Thin stray stems back to a side branch within the canopy. Shear for formal plantings or prune hard in early summer. Treat inkberry (*I. glabra*) and yaupon (*I. vomitoria*) the same way.
Thin in late winter; shear in early to midsummer	Thin out multiple leaders and stray or damaged branches. Clip or shear hedges annually. When cutting for holiday decoration, maintain shape and balance. Treat English holly (*I. aquifolium*) and Burford Chinese holly (*I. cornuta* 'Burfordii') the same. Don't overprune pyramidal hollies such as 'Nellie R. Stevens', *I. × aquipernyi* 'San Jose', and American holly (*I. opaca*).
Late winter to early spring	Keep compact by digging out unwanted suckers; renew straggly plants by cutting back one-quarter to one-third of the oldest, thickest, tallest stems over three or four years.

BOTANICAL NAME	COMMON NAME	HABIT	SHAPE	PRUNING METHODS	
Jasminum nudiflorum	WINTER JASMINE	Deciduous shrub or ground cover	Spreading	Sucker removal, renovating, espalier	
Jasminum officinale	HARDY JASMINE, POET'S JASMINE	Semi-evergreen twining vine	Vine	Cleanup, shaping, pinching	
Juniperus spp.	JUNIPER	Evergreen ground covers, shrubs, or columnar trees	Mat, spreading, or columnar	Limbing up, cleanup, espalier (*J. × pfitzeriana*)	
Kadsura japonica	KADSURA	Evergreen to semi-evergreen twining vine	Vine	Shaping	
Kalmia latifolia	MOUNTAIN LAUREL	Broadleaf evergreen shrub	Rounded to irregular	Thinning, pinching, deadheading, renewal	

TIME	PRUNING TIPS
After bloom	Aggressive spreader. Leave trailing stems for plants to mound and spread, or cut and transplant rooted stems. Rejuvenate gangly plants by cutting to the ground every five or so years.
After bloom	Blooms on old wood and also new growth at tips. Prune immediately after bloom to keep in check; remove dead wood and side branches that have flowered. Grow as a flowering hedge by pinching growing tips for bushiness, thinning out weak or damaged stems, and heading back upright stems to a healthy outside bud.
When dormant or as needed	Needs little pruning; remove dead or interfering branches. Cut to a section with live foliage so new growth can resprout. If you must remove a branch, cut back to another branch or branch collar at the trunk.
Late winter to early spring	Needs training and thinning to control growth. Remove winter damage and stray stems.
After bloom	Needs little pruning when well sited. For maximum flowers or tidiness, deadhead right after bloom. For more compact or shorter bush, cut back longest stems to side branches. Renew old, overgrown plants.

BOTANICAL NAME	COMMON NAME	HABIT	SHAPE	PRUNING METHODS	
Kerria japonica	JAPANESE KERRIA	Deciduous shrub	Rounded, suckering	Thinning, sucker removal, renewal, cleanup	
Koelreuteria paniculata	GOLDEN RAIN TREE	Deciduous flowering tree	Vase to rounded	Training, cleanup	
Kolkwitzia amabilis	BEAUTY-BUSH	Deciduous shrub	Rounded, spreading	Thinning, cleanup, renewal, renovating	
Laburnum × watereri 'Vossii'	GOLDEN-CHAIN TREE	Deciduous tree	Oval to rounded	Training, sucker removal, cleanup	
Lagerstroemia indica	CRAPE MYRTLE	Deciduous shrub or small tree	Rounded	Deadheading, sucker removal, cleanup, renovating, shrub-to-tree, espalier	
Larix spp.	LARCH	Needled deciduous trees	Pyramidal	Cleanup	

TIME	PRUNING TIPS
After bloom	Remove winterkill in spring; cut dead branches to the ground. Blooms best and produces most vivid foliage when old flowering stems are thinned to fresh shoots. Control spread by digging out unwanted suckers. Renew over three years.
Late winter to early spring	Train for well-spaced branches and central leader. Prune out dead branches. Invasive self-sower; dig out seedlings around tree.
After bloom	Thin old flowering stems for compactness without altering basic arching shape. Leggy with age; renovate by cutting stems to 6 in. or cut back one-third of oldest, thickest stems each year.
After bloom	Train for a strong form. Prune off dead, diseased, and broken branches. Avoid pruning big branches from old trees if possible, as cuts are slow to heal. Snip any suckers emerging from the rootstock.
Late winter to early spring	Blooms on new wood. To keep shrubby, prune to 6 in. before new growth begins. Deadheading cultivars that bloom before mid-July encourages a second, sometimes third flush of bloom. Removing big live limbs on mature bushes stimulates growth of floppy shoots, so train to tree form early and cut out dead or crossing branches and suckers promptly.
Late winter to early spring	Remove dead, broken, or diseased branches. On big trees, low branches may be shaded out and die. Sweeping low stems of some larches layer on ground to form new plants; remove (or allow weeping cultivars to spread as undulating ground cover).

BOTANICAL NAME	COMMON NAME	HABIT	SHAPE	PRUNING METHODS	
Laurus nobilis	BAY LAUREL, SWEET BAY	Evergreen shrub or single-trunk tree	Pyramidal	Topiary, espalier, shear, prune as standard, root pruning	
Lavandula angustifolia	ENGLISH LAVENDER	Evergreen shrub, often grown as a perennial	Rounded	Pinch, shear, prune as standard	
Lespedeza thunbergii	BUSH CLOVER	Deciduous shrub	Rounded	Renovating	
Ligustrum spp.	PRIVET	Deciduous, evergreen, semi-evergreen shrubs and trees	Oval to spreading	Shearing, topiary	
Liquidambar styraciflua	SWEET GUM	Deciduous tree	Oval to pyramidal	Training, cleanup, limbing up	
Liriodendron tulipifera	TULIP TREE	Deciduous tree	Pyramidal	Training, thinning, cleanup, limbing up	

TIME	PRUNING TIPS
Late winter to early spring; midsummer	Shape any time during growing period; dormant pruning stimulates most growth. To grow as a tree, keep lower side branches cut off. In pots, clip branches and root-prune or repot as needed.
Early spring	Pruning maintains vigor and compactness. Starting when young, cut back by one-third to one-half each year before new growth starts or pinch tips to promote branching. Cutting into bare wood can kill a branch.
Late winter to early spring	Blooms on new wood; dies back in winter. Cut to the ground each year before new growth begins.
Early spring, as needed during growing season	Cut new plants back hard in early spring for a couple of years after planting. Shear frequently to keep rapid growth tidy. In spring, rejuvenate old hedges by clipping tops and sides way back.
Late winter to early spring	Grows with straight trunk; prune to space branches. Can limb up for textured bark. Keep away from walks, as roots can heave up sidewalks.
Late winter to early spring	Fast-growing, somewhat brittle wood; keep away from house because of branch drop, particularly in storms. Train for strong branch attachments; thin out dead, weak, damaged limbs. Limb up heavy low branches to show powerful, elegant trunk.

BOTANICAL NAME	COMMON NAME	HABIT	SHAPE	PRUNING METHODS	
Lonicera sempervirens	CORAL HONEY-SUCKLE	Deciduous twining vine	Vine	Shaping	
Loropetalum chinense	LOROPETA-LUM	Broadleaf evergreen to semi-evergreen shrub or small tree	Rounded	Thinning, shrub-to-tree, shearing, espalier	
Macfadyena unguis-cati	CAT'S-CLAW CREEPER	Evergreen clinging vine	Vine	Shaping	
Magnolia spp.	MAGNOLIA	Deciduous shrubs, deciduous or ever-green trees (depends on species)	Oval, rounded, or pyra-midal (depends on species)	Training, sucker removal, cleanup	
Mahonia aquifolium	MAHONIA, OREGON GRAPE HOLLY	Broadleaf evergreen shrub	Rounded to spreading	Reno-vating, cleanup, sucker removal	
Malus spp.	FLOWERING CRAB APPLE	Deciduous small trees	Rounded	Training, thinning, cleanup, sucker removal, shearing	

TIME	PRUNING TIPS
After bloom	Needs little pruning. Snip stray stems to shape after blooming. Unlike weedy, invasive Japanese honeysuckle (*L. japonica*), this native behaves well.
After bloom	Needs little pruning or shaping unless grown as formal hedge or espalier. Tolerates hard pruning and regular shearing. Turn into ground cover by cutting out upright stems.
After bloom	Prune to keep from growing too fast and becoming thin at base. Trim after bloom to encourage bushy growth habit.
After bloom	Seldom needs pruning beyond shaping for a strong form in early years; remove dead and damaged branches. Dig out suckers from rootstock as soon as they appear. Avoid making large cuts if possible; cut ends may not heal well.
After bloom	Doesn't need much pruning when given adequate space. To restrict natural spread, remove suckers. Renovate if it grows leggy over time.
After bloom	Train to central leader. Get rid of suckers when they appear. Clip lightly for an informal hedge or frequently and severely for a more formal look. Prickly varieties such as 'Robusta' make good barrier hedges if sheared heavily in early summer for thick bottom growth. Some forms ('Red Jade', 'Mary Potter', 'Sargentii') fruit in alternate years; cut off some flowers during abundant years to encourage annual fruiting.

BOTANICAL NAME	COMMON NAME	HABIT	SHAPE	PRUNING METHODS	
Myrica pensylvanica	BAYBERRY	Deciduous to semi-evergreen shrub	Rounded, suckering	Sucker removal, cleanup, shrub-to-tree	
Nandina domestica	HEAVENLY BAMBOO	Broadleaf evergreen shrub	Rounded to spreading	Thinning	
Nerium oleander	OLEANDER	Broadleaf evergreen shrub	Rounded	Thinning, shearing, shrub-to-tree, prune as standard, espalier	
Nyssa sylvatica	BLACK GUM	Deciduous tree	Spreading (somewhat pyramidal when young)	Cleanup, limbing up	
Osmanthus heterophyllus	HOLLY TEA OLIVE, FALSE HOLLY	Broadleaf evergreen shrub	Rounded	Thinning, renovating	
Oxydendrum arboreum	SOURWOOD	Deciduous tree	Pyramidal	Training, cleanup	
Paeonia suffruticosa	TREE PEONY	Deciduous shrub	Rounded	Deadheading, sucker removal, cleanup	

TIME	PRUNING TIPS
Early spring, cleanup at any time	Little pruning beyond cleanup. Remove suckers to control spread. Can train into a small tree.
Late winter to early spring	To keep attractive and compact, cut back some old stems to the ground every year.
After bloom	Reduce legginess by thinning tallest stems in late winter. To train into a tree, choose a few strong stems and remove suckers and bottom growth, or choose one stem for a flowering standard. Attractive hedge or espalier. Wear gloves when pruning, since contact with sap may cause an allergic reaction.
Late winter to early spring	Doesn't need much beyond cleanup. If planted near a path, limb up to make some room underneath.
After bloom, early spring	Resprouts on old wood. For an informal hedge, thin long shoots back to larger branches within the shrubs. Rejuvenate by hard pruning in early spring.
Late winter to early spring	Train to a central leader when young. Rarely needs anything else.
After bloom	Grows well with little pruning. Sometimes grafted, so remove basal suckers. Remove dead branches when shrub is in leaf.

BOTANICAL NAME	COMMON NAME	HABIT	SHAPE	PRUNING METHODS	
Parthenocissus spp.	VIRGINIA CREEPER, WOODBINE, BOSTON IVY	Deciduous clinging vines or ground covers	Vine	Shaping, cleanup	
Passiflora spp.	PASSION-FLOWER	Evergreen to semi-evergreen clinging vines	Vine	Shaping, pinching	
Paulownia tomentosa	PRINCESS TREE, EMPRESS TREE	Deciduous tree	Rounded	Training, coppicing	
Phellodendron amurense	AMUR CORK TREE	Deciduous tree	Spreading	Training	
Philadelphus coronarius	SWEET MOCK ORANGE	Deciduous shrub	Rounded	Thinning, renovating, cleanup	
Photinia × *fraseri*	REDTIP, FRASER PHOTINIA	Broadleaf evergreen shrub or tree	Oval	Thinning, heading back, cleanup, shearing, shrub-to-tree, renovating	

TIME	PRUNING TIPS
Any time	Need pruning to keep under control; remove dead and damaged material. Trim stray growth to a bud or shoot in the direction you want it to grow. Thin to reduce weight if too heavy for arch or trellis.
Late winter to early spring	Bloom on new wood. For the best show, plant in full sun and prune annually to keep an open habit.
Late winter to early spring	Fast growing and weak-wooded; train early for strong form. Coppice for a bold garden accent; this prevents tree from flowering and fruiting and renders harmless a messy, invasive tree.
Late winter to early spring	Train to a straight central leader. Invasive in many areas.
After bloom, early spring to renovate	Leggy and awkward unless pruned. Cut down some old, tall stems after flowering each year. Remove weak crossing branches, head back leggy or drooping branches, clip off all suckers. Cutting neglected shrubs to the ground in late winter or early spring removes current season's blooms but produces strong regrowth.
Late winter to midsummer	Tolerates drastic pruning; each shearing produces red new growth, but stop after midsummer to prevent winter injury. Head back stray branches to a larger branch or strong bud within canopy; thin out dead and diseased growth. Prune young hedges hard for low branching.

BOTANICAL NAME	COMMON NAME	HABIT	SHAPE	PRUNING METHODS	
Physocarpus opulifolius	NINEBARK	Deciduous shrub	Rounded to spreading	Renovating, thinning, cleanup, shearing	
Picea spp.	SPRUCE	Needled evergreen trees	Pyramidal	Candling, shearing, cleanup	
Pieris spp.	ANDROM-EDA	Broadleaf evergreen shrubs	Rounded	Thinning, renovating	
Pinus spp.	PINE	Narrow-leafed evergreen shrubs or trees	Pyramidal, rounded, or spreading	Candling, shearing	
Pittosporum tobira	JAPANESE MOCK ORANGE	Broadleaf evergreen shrub	Rounded to vase	Thinning, shearing, shrub-to-tree	
Platanus × hispanica	LONDON PLANE TREE	Deciduous tree	Pyramidal to rounded	Training, cleanup, limbing up	

TIME	PRUNING TIPS
Late winter to early spring	Cut out dead, damaged, diseased material. Maintain size and shape by cutting back stems to healthy out-facing buds or shoots within crown. Plant dwarf varieties to minimize shearing of hedges. Renew gangly specimens by cutting to the ground when dormant.
Late winter to early spring for major pruning, light pruning any time	Bottom branches may die with age; remove as needed. For a tighter look or dense hedge, start shearing when young. Shear only young growth; cutting into bare wood below needles can kill a branch. Choose a variety that will grow to the height you want. Colorado blue spruce varies from bright green to blue-white, so choose hedge plants of uniform color.
After bloom	Cut back overly long shoots to outward growing bud or branch inside crown. If badly winter-damaged or overgrown, rejuvenate in late winter by pruning to 6 to 12 in. from the ground.
Late winter to early spring for heavy pruning	To control growth, twist off soft new growth (candles) in late spring or early summer, before it hardens. When shearing, cut only new growth. Pruning into bare wood can kill branches.
After bloom; major pruning in early spring	Tolerates hard pruning to old wood in early spring. Limb up for attractive single or multi-stemmed tree. Formal hedge requires multiple shearings, which destroys flowers.
Late winter to early spring	Cut out competing leaders when they occur. Remove dead, diseased, and damaged material. Limb up to enjoy showy, flaking bark.

BOTANICAL NAME	COMMON NAME	HABIT	SHAPE	PRUNING METHODS	
Podocarpus chinensis	YEW PINE, JAPANESE YEW	Evergreen needled shrub or tree	Columnar	Shearing, renovating	
Populus nigra 'Italica'	LOMBARDY POPLAR	Deciduous tree	Columnar	Cleanup	
Potentilla fruticosa	SHRUBBY CINQUEFOIL	Deciduous shrub	Spreading	Thinning, shearing, renovating, renewal	
Prunus spp.	FLOWERING CHERRY, CHERRY, PLUM, APRICOT, ALMOND, PEACH	Deciduous trees	Rounded, vase, or oval	Cleanup, heading back, shearing	
Prunus × cistena	PURPLE-LEAF SAND CHERRY	Deciduous shrub	Rounded	Thinning, cleanup, shrub-to-tree	
Prunus laurocerasus	CHERRY LAUREL	Broadleaf evergreen shrub or small tree	Rounded, spreading	Thinning, renewal	

TIME	PRUNING TIPS
Late winter to early spring (major pruning); clip or shear as needed	Low-maintenance hedge or foundation plant. Shear regularly to maintain desired form. To renovate, cut to ground in late winter or early spring.
Late summer	Naturally strong form but needs replacing in a few years because of disease and pest infestations. Most poplars are fast growing, weak-wooded, and short-lived.
Late winter to early spring	Unpruned plants may get scraggly; remove wayward stems or shear lightly with hand clippers for a tighter look. Renew by cutting half the stems to the ground and the remaining half the second year. Or renovate, if the bush is vigorous.
After bloom	Remove dead, diseased, damaged, and crossing branches from late spring to summer, when disease spores are least active. For an informal barrier, clip native plums lightly or shear as needed. For fruit production, see chapter 11.
After bloom	Tolerates hard pruning. Remove dead, diseased, and damaged branches from late spring to summer, when disease spores are least active.
After bloom	Cut back branches to a side bud or branch; avoid shearing, which damages the handsome, shiny green leaves. Renew by cutting back branches over several years. Prune in late spring or summer, when bacterial canker spores are inactive. Treat Carolina cherry laurel (*P. caroliniana*) the same.

BOTANICAL NAME	COMMON NAME	HABIT	SHAPE	PRUNING METHODS	
Punica granatum	POME-GRANATE	Deciduous shrub	Rounded	Thinning, sucker removal, espalier, shrub-to-tree	
Pyracantha coccinea	FIRETHORN	Broadleaf evergreen to semi-evergreen shrub	Spreading	Espalier, thinning, cleanup, shearing	
Pyrus calleryana	ORNAMEN-TAL PEAR	Deciduous tree	Pyramidal	Training, cleanup	
Quercus spp.	OAK	Deciduous trees	Rounded to spread-ing (with age)	Training, cleanup	
Rhododendron spp.	RHODO-DENDRON, AZALEA	Decidu-ous or evergreen shrubs	Vase to rounded or spread-ing (depends on cultivar)	Cleanup, pinch-ing, dead-heading, thinning, renewal, renovating	

TIME	PRUNING TIPS
Early spring	Blooms on new growth; prune when dormant. Remove suckers from roots and trunks. Can train to one or more trunks for a small tree or as a fan-shaped espalier.
Late winter to early spring (major pruning); after bloom (light pruning)	Thin out dead, damaged, and crossing branches to improve air circulation and encourage denser growth. Tolerates hard pruning, which reduces fruits the following growing season. Burn or bury diseased branches. Wear gloves because spines may cause an allergic reaction.
Late winter to early spring (major pruning); after bloom (light pruning)	Upright limbs and very narrow branch crotches often result in large chunks of crown breaking off. Open-branched cultivar 'Aristocrat' is less prone to wind damage. Remove limbs affected by fire blight and other diseases; bag or burn prunings.
When dormant	Limit pruning to training when young and to removing dead, diseased, and broken wood; avoid making large cuts. Prune only when dormant, which is late winter to early spring for deciduous oaks and July through October for live oaks.
After bloom, rejuvenate in late winter to early spring	For a tight, compact bush, pinch or cut back young plants; remove an inch or so of new growth above a set of leaves. Each year deadhead (except types with small blooms) and cut out dead, diseased, and damaged wood. Renew or renovate older, overgrown bushes; cut ¼ to ½ in. above an outward-facing bud.

BOTANICAL NAME	COMMON NAME	HABIT	SHAPE	PRUNING METHODS	
Rosa spp.	ROSE	Deciduous shrubs	Rounded or suckering	Cleanup, thinning, dead-heading, heading back, renewal (depends on type)	
Rosmarinus officinalis	ROSEMARY	Evergreen shrub or ground cover	Rounded or mat (depends on cultivar)	Cleanup, shearing, pruning as standard, topiary	
Rubus odoratus	FLOWERING RASPBERRY	Deciduous shrub	Spreading, suckering	Sucker removal, cleanup	
Salix × sepulcralis 'Chrysocoma'	GOLDEN WEEPING WILLOW	Deciduous tree	Weeping	Training, cleanup	
Sambucus spp.	ELDER-BERRY	Deciduous shrubs	Rounded, suckering	Thinning, renovat-ing, sucker removal	
Schisandra chinensis	SCHISAN-DRA, MAG-NOLIA VINE	Deciduous twining vine	Vine	Shaping	
Sorbus spp.	MOUNTAIN ASH	Deciduous trees	Oval to rounded	Training, cleanup	

TIME	PRUNING TIPS
Late winter to midsummer (depends on type)	Remove weak, crossing branches and head back to encourage denser growth. In cold climates, wait until after last frost to prune. Cut older canes right after bloom. To shorten tall, floppy shrub roses, cut back all leggy branches and thin out all suckers and a few older branches. Disbud for larger blooms. See Roses in chapter 6.
Any time; after bloom for best flowering	Tolerates drastic pruning. Harvest at any time. Prune after bloom to promote pretty little blue, pink, or white flowers.
After fruiting	Control suckers to restrict spread.
Summer	Prune and stake early to prevent weeping when too young, which creates a misshapen bush instead of a graceful tree. Shorten branches dragging on the ground. Avoid overpruning, which stimulates too much regrowth. Dormant pruning causes sap to run but does not harm tree.
Late winter to early spring	For denser, bushier growth or to control size, prune whole shrub back hard in early spring. Remove suckers to control spread.
Late winter to early spring	Needs only light pruning. Flowers on old wood. Prune when dormant to maximize display of showy edible fruit.
Late winter to early spring	Train for strong form, eliminating weak crotches.

BOTANICAL NAME	COMMON NAME	HABIT	SHAPE	PRUNING METHODS	
Spiraea spp.	SPIREA	Deciduous shrubs	Rounded, spreading	Thinning, renewal, deadheading, heading back,	
Symphoricarpos spp.	SNOW-BERRY, CORAL-BERRY	Deciduous shrubs	Spreading, suckering	Sucker removal, thinning	
Symplocos paniculata	SWEET-LEAF, SAPPHIRE BERRY	Deciduous shrub or small tree	Spreading	Thinning, renewal	
Syringa spp.	LILAC	Deciduous shrubs or trees	Spreading, rounded or oval (depends on species)	Thinning, deadheading, sucker removal, cleanup, renewal	
Taxodium spp.	BALD CYPRESS	Needled deciduous trees	Pyramidal	Cleanup	
Taxus spp.	YEW	Needled evergreen shrubs or trees	Pyramidal, columnar, or spreading (depends on variety)	Pinching, shearing, renovating	

TIME	PRUNING TIPS
Late winter to early spring or after bloom (depends on species)	Prune spring bloomers (bridal wreath, *S. prunifolia*, and *S. nipponica* 'Snowmound') right after flowering. Prune later-blooming Japanese (*S. japonica*) and Billiard spirea (*S.* × *billiardii*) in late winter or very early spring. To control size and shape, head back by one-third to a new bud or shoot and cut back some old growth to the ground. To prevent unwanted seedlings (especially *S. japonica*), deadhead after bloom.
Late winter to early spring	Bloom on new wood. Remove suckers to control spread. Grow leggy with age; thin out some stems each year and cut back others by one-third to one-half.
After bloom or after fruit withers	Slow grower; needs little pruning. Prune to shape; renew old bushes. To fully enjoy berries, postpone pruning until they lose their charm.
After bloom	Cut off fading blooms. Remove weak and crossing branches. Some are grafted; prune or pull out foreign-looking sprouts before they take over (see page 101). Japanese tree lilac (*S. reticulata*) can be grown as a large shrub or tree; needs little pruning.
Late winter to early spring	Naturally sturdy structure. Remove dead and broken branches. Cut back to a healthy bud branches affected by twig blight fungus.
Early summer	Tolerate heavy pruning because they regrow on old wood. Shear once or twice during the growing season.

BOTANICAL NAME	COMMON NAME	HABIT	SHAPE	PRUNING METHODS	
Teucrium chamaedrys	WALL GERMANDER	Evergreen shrub or ground cover	Rounded	Shaping, shearing	
Thuja spp.	ARBORVI-TAE	Evergreen shrubs or trees	Oval or pyramidal	Shearing, thinning	
Tilia spp.	LINDEN, BASSWOOD	Deciduous trees	Oval	Training, cleanup, limbing up, sucker removal	
Trache-lospermum jasminoides	STAR JAS-MINE, CON-FEDERATE JASMINE	Evergreen twining vine	Vine	Shaping, shearing	
Tsuga spp.	HEMLOCK	Needled evergreen trees	Pyramidal	Shearing, thinning, cleanup	
Ulmus parvifolia	LACEBARK ELM, CHI-NESE ELM	Deciduous tree	Rounded	Training, limbing up	
Vaccinium spp.	BLUEBERRY	Deciduous shrubs	Rounded	Thinning, cleanup	

TIME	PRUNING TIPS
Late winter to early spring	Keep bushy through shearing or clipping.
Early summer (shearing)	Produce new growth on old wood. Prune hedges in early summer; take off individual branch to a bud or branch at any time. Choose pyramidal types for tall, narrow hedge that needs shearing only on top.
Late winter to early spring	Train to single leader with well-spaced branches. Remove basal suckers and dead, diseased, and broken wood. Remove lower limbs to show the distinctive ridged bark.
After bloom	Seldom needs pruning. Shear for 2-ft. ground cover.
Early summer (shearing); single branches any time	Withstands heavy pruning but is best left natural. Trim individual branches any time. Prune dead and dying branches from adelgid-infested plants to stimulate new growth and help tree resist further damage.
Late winter to early spring	Grow naturally with multiple trunks or train to single trunk. Limb up to showcase the bark.
Late winter to early spring	Lowbush blueberry (*V. angustifolium*) needs little care; cut out dead wood when necessary. For highbush blueberry (*V. corymbosum*), remove old, weak, dead, damaged, and unproductive wood; shorten branches that bend over. For fruit production, see chapter 12.

BOTANICAL NAME	COMMON NAME	HABIT	SHAPE	PRUNING METHODS	
Viburnum spp.	VIBURNUM	Deciduous, semi-evergreen, or evergreen shrubs or trees	Oval, rounded, spreading, or suckering (depends on species)	Cleanup, thinning, renewal, shrub-to-tree (depends on species)	
Vitex agnus-castus	CHASTE TREE, HEMP TREE	Deciduous shrub or small multi-trunk tree	Vase to spreading	Thinning, shrub-to-tree, limbing up	
Vitis spp.	GRAPE	Deciduous clinging vines	Vine	Shaping	
Weigela spp.	WEIGELA	Deciduous shrubs	Rounded	Thinning, cleanup	
Wisteria spp.	WISTERIA	Deciduous twining vines	Vine	Shaping, sucker removal, pinching	
Zelkova serrata	JAPANESE ZELKOVA	Deciduous tree	Vase	Training, cleanup	

TIME	PRUNING TIPS
After bloom	Blooms on old wood. Shape lightly right after blooming; do heavy pruning in late winter. Remove crossing branches, thin out some old wood, and head back some small branches to revive earlier blooming and bearing vigor. Encourage annual berry crop by cutting off some flowers during years when shrub blooms heavily.
Late winter to early spring	Blooms on new wood. In a smaller space, train to a single trunk.
Late winter to early spring	When grown as an ornamental, prune only to keep under control. For fruit production, see chapter 12.
After bloom	May need heavy pruning to get rid of dead wood and winter injury. Head back old and damaged branches to a vigorous outward bud or shoot.
Early spring, summer	In late winter to early spring, cut back to visible framework, leaving about four buds per stem; in summer, thin out all unwanted stems and cut back other new shoots to several inches. Or grow as large bush by cutting and pinching vinelike tendrils as they grow. Often grafted, so remove suckers, which can crowd out the grafted plant. Support with stakes for the first 10 years.
Late winter to early spring	Train to correct multiple leaders and weak crotches unless you buy a well-formed tree with well-spaced branches. Remove dead or dying material promptly; don't compost prunings.

Index

Page numbers in **bold** indicate
illustrations.

Other Storey Titles You Will Enjoy

Christmas Trees, by Lewis Hill.
Complete, clear information on the basics of growing and
selling trees, wreaths, and greens.
160 pages. Paper. ISBN 978-0-88266-566-5.

The Homeowner's Complete Tree & Shrub Handbook,
by Penny O'Sullivan.
The new bible of tree and shrub selection and care, showing
hundreds of plant possibilities in full-color photographs.
416 pages. Paper. ISBN 978-1-58017-570-8.
Hardcover with jacket. ISBN 978-1-58017-571-5.

Landscaping with Fruit, by Lee Reich.
A complete, accessible guide to luscious landscaping — from
alpine strawberry to lingonberry, mulberry to wintergreen.
192 pages. Paper. ISBN 978-1-60342-091-4.
Hardcover with jacket. ISBN 978-1-60342-096-9.

The Organic Lawn Care Manual, by Paul Tukey.
A comprehensive volume of natural lawn-care information to
answer the growing demand for organic grass.
272 pages. Paper. ISBN 978-1-58017-649-1.
Hardcover. ISBN 978-1-58017-655-2.

The Veggie Gardener's Answer Book, by Barbara W. Ellis.
Insider's tips and tricks, practical advice, and organic wisdom
for vegetable growers everywhere.
432 pages. Flexibind. ISBN 978-1-60342-024-2.

These and other books from Storey Publishing are available
wherever quality books are sold or by calling 1-800-441-5700.
Visit us at *www.storey.com*.